KT-418-866

Skills-based Learning for Caring for a Loved One with an Eating Disorder

The new Maudsley method

Janet Treasure, Gráinne Smith
and Anna Crane

Routledge
Taylor & Francis Group

LONDON AND NEW YORK

NORWICH CITY COLLEGE

Stock No.	231 711		
Class	616.85 TRE		
Cat.	3.ıc	Proc	SSA2

First published 2007
by Routledge
27 Church Road, Hove, East Sussex BN3 2FA

Simultaneously published in the USA and Canada
by Routledge
270 Madison Avenue, New York NY 10016

Reprinted 2008 (twice), 2009 (twice) and 2010

Routledge is an imprint of the Taylor & Francis Group, an Informa business

© 2007 Janet Treasure, Gráinne Smith and Anna Crane

Typeset in Scala Sans by RefineCatch Limited, Bungay, Suffolk
Cartoons by Gary Holmes
Printed and bound in Great Britain by TJ International Ltd, Padstow, Cornwall
Cover design by Anú Design

All rights reserved. No part of this book may be reprinted or
reproduced or utilized in any form or by any electronic,
mechanical, or other means, now known or hereafter
invented, including photocopying and recording, or in any
information storage or retrieval system, without permission in
writing from the publishers.

British Library Cataloguing in Publication Data
A catalogue record for this book is available from the British Library

Library of Congress Cataloging-in-Publication Data
Treasure, Janet
Skills-based learning for caring for a loved one with an eating disorder: the new
Maudsley method / Janet Treasure, Gráinne Smith, and Anna Crane.
p. cm.
Includes bibliographical references and index.
ISBN-13: 978-0-415-43158-3 (pbk.)
ISBN-10: 0-415-43158-1 (pbk.)
1. Eating disorders.   2. Caregivers.   I. Smith, Gráinne, 1945–
II. Crane, Anna.   III. Title.
RC552.E18T738 2007
616.85′26 – dc22

20060100294

ISBN: 978-0-415-43158-3 (pbk)

Contents

Preface

Why Have We Written this Manual?

1. Eating disorder symptoms have a profound impact on other people as well as the person with the eating disorder. The impact that this has on carers has often been neglected.

2. Automatic reactions to these symptoms may not be the most helpful.

3. Taking a step back to reflect on the most effective way to manage symptoms can lessen the adverse impact on you as a family and the individual him- or herself.

4. Our work with carers suggests that several 'C' words can be useful cues to keep in mind: calmness, communication, compassion, cooperation, consistency and coaching.

5. Practical skills helpful in home management are the same as those used by professionals on specialised eating disorders units, such as the Maudsley.

6. This book therefore gives you skills and information about working with the current Maudsley method.

Over many years, our ward teams at the Maudsley have developed vast expertise and skills in dealing with eating disorder sufferers. Our aim is to summarise and share some of this information. We hope that you too can become competent in helping someone with an eating disorder to recover.

FACT – *As a carer you CAN have a role preventing the illness retaining its hold over an individual's life. This manual may provide you with the know-how.*

Who Are We?

Janet Treasure is a psychiatrist who has worked professionally with people with eating disorders for over 25 years at the Eating Disorder Unit at the South London and Maudsley Hospital NHS Trust, which is a leading centre in clinical management and training of eating disorders. She was chairman of the physical treatment section of the UK NICE guideline committee. She is the Chief Medical Advisor for *beat* (the main UK eating disorder charity) and is the trustee of the Sheffield eating disorders association.

Gráinne Smith is a carer who has for many years run a helpline for carers in Scotland and beyond. She has written a book for carers of people with eating disorders, and has worked with the Institute of Psychiatry (IOP), King's College, London team developing a web-based programme for carers. She is a member of the Patient/Carer task force of the Academy of Eating Disorders and a co-author of the Academy's Charter for Patients and Carers.

Anna Crane is a medical student at King's College, London and has personal experience of an eating disorder. She has written about her experiences in the *Student BMJ* (studentbmj.com). She has developed materials for increasing eating disorder awareness.

Who Can Help? Who Is a Carer?

The word carer is used throughout this book to mean any home carer or a parent. In the main parents take on this role in the community but partners and siblings also have an invaluable role to play. The content of this book applies to any individual in a care-giving relationship with someone with an eating disorder, both professional and non-professional.

As the information in this book is used for staff training at the specialised eating disorder unit at the Maudsley Hospital, at times the style of the book may not fit exactly with carers' individual situations. Carers may need to adapt the information through discussion before use. However, the broad concepts for practical care, whether in a ward or home situation, are relevant.

What Is the Problem?

It is difficult to know what terms to use to describe such an illness. Each case has individual features. Some people advocate using specific terms – anorexia nervosa or bulimia nervosa – but an individual can move in and out and between these different forms at different stages. Therefore, it may be easier to use the broad term 'eating disorder'.

In writing of these illnesses, it often feels awkward to repeatedly write 'the individual with the eating disorder' or 'your loved one' or 'your daughter, son or spouse'. Rather than use any of these, 'Edi' is used as a name to represent any eating disordered individual throughout this manual. 'Edi' may be male or female and of any age but, as a carer, substitute your own loved one's name for Edi.

Eating disorders, by their nature, are characterised by extreme and complex behaviours. Trying to come to terms with such behaviour is a huge challenge for carers. Using 'Edi' as a name, instead of William, Sarah, Emily, Laura, etc., may help separate this unacceptable behaviour (sometimes referred to as the 'anorexic minx'!) from the person with an eating disorder.

How Can You Use this Training Material?

The manual consists of a series of 14 chapters each of which addresses a particular topic pertinent to the care of an eating disorder sufferer. Chapter 1 is useful information for the sufferer themselves. Each chapter starts with an introduction to the theoretical element of the topic. From there, with the help of examples and tasks, the aim of the manual is to guide the carer through the challenges and issues commonly arising, in our experience, from their role. An '**Action Points**' box donates suggestions of practical exercises relevant to the chapter whilst a '**Reflections Points**' box summarises important 'take home' messages to contemplate. Some chapters are in the form of 'Skills' sheets which can be worked through or 'dipped' in and out of. Other chapters are more theoretical in their basis.

It is not easy to attain the skills we describe in the manual. As part of our research endeavours we have offered various supplements, workshops, telephone coaching and DVDs. Workshops allow for interactive reflections and questions and the opportunity to put newfound knowledge and skills into practice with role play and demonstration. Living with someone with an eating disorder is often a lonely and isolating experience. Workshops allow for carers to share problems, learn from each other and, most importantly, to appreciate that they are not alone. Please go to our website to get further information.

It is up to each individual how they choose to work through the manual. Some may like to skim read the whole text first, going back to relevant chapters pertinent to their situation at the time. Others may prefer to methodically work through each chapter in succession, absorbing each skill in turn. The choice is yours.

Will It Work?

Learning these skills is a tough assignment. It is usual to build these techniques from a background in psychological theory, and practical experience in the mental health field. Nevertheless, the feedback that we have from families is that they welcome having structure and theory to guide them, as sometimes what seems common sense – simply trying to encourage someone to eat a healthy diet – may not help. Most carers find these skills are valuable, not only for managing eating disorders, but also in a wider arena, at home and at work.

Tips to Success

(1) Practice and Reflection

Practice and reflection are two fundamental components to successfully using this manual. *It cannot be emphasised enough how important it is to practise, reflect and then practise again.* The training of a professional therapist takes years and involves continued support sessions in the form of tutorials with other more experienced professionals (known as 'supervision'). Training requires listening to audio or videotapes of performances and the constant reflection, analysis and documentation of progress and errors. Obviously, this is not easy to transfer to the home situation . . . Try to set aside time to reflect on your progress. If possible, ask for feedback from your partner, from a relative or friend, and from the person with the eating disorder – Edi. Is it possible to get some supervision or support from other carers, perhaps through a self-help group?

(2) The Process

This training package will help you to appreciate that it is the process – *how* and *what* you do – rather than any single outcome from an interaction that is important. Keep this in mind.

(3) 'Every Mistake is a Treasure'

Vitally important to remember. Do not let high personal standards or perfectionism cramp your new style. Throughout the manual, you will be reminded of this.

And Finally

It is not possible to give examples of every problem you might encounter, but we hope that you can adapt some of the broad models that we give you.

We have developed this booklet with the help of many carers who have told us what their needs are and what works and does not work. There may be errors, so please accept our apologies for these. We are always interested to improve on what we have done. One way you can help in this process is by joining the Carers Volunteer Database. To join, email edu@iop.kcl.ac.uk

Good luck!

Further Information and Useful Resources

Books

The following list is not exhaustive but gives examples written to give help and advice to carers:

Bloomfield, S. (ed.) *Eating disorders: Helping your child recover*, Norwich, UK: EDA, 2006.

Bryant-Waugh, R. and Lask, B. *Eating disorders: A parent's guide*. Hove, East Sussex: Brunner-Routledge, 1999.

Collins, L. *Eating with your anorexic: How my child recovered through family based treatment and yours can too*. New York, NY: McGraw-Hill, 2005.

Crisp, A.H., Joughin, N., Halek, C. and Bowyer, C. *Anorexia nervosa: The wish to change*. Hove, East Sussex: Psychology Press, 1996.

Department of Health. *A national service framework for mental health*. London: Department of Health, 1999.

Natenshon, A.H. *When your child has an eating disorder*. San Francisco, CA: Jossey-Bass Inc., 1999.

Schmidt, U. and Treasure, J. *Getting better bit(e) by bit(e): A survival kit for sufferers of bulimia nervosa and binge eating disorders*. Hove, East Sussex: Brunner-Routledge, 1993.

Smith, G. *Anorexia and bulimia in the family*. Chichester, UK: Wiley, 2004.

Treasure, J. *Anorexia nervosa: A survival guide for sufferers and those caring for someone with an eating disorder*. Hove, East Sussex: Psychology Press, 1997.

Guidelines on Websites

The IOP website with links to the Maudsley website www.eating
research.com has a section with information for carers which may
be of help. It also has sections for professionals, and users.

Specific Eating Disorder Organisations

beat (beating eating disorders)   www.b-eat.co.uk
USA Eating Disorders Association   www.nationaleatingdisorders.org
Academy for Eating Disorders
    (AED is an international
    transdisciplinary
    professional organisation)   www.aedweb.org/

General Carers Information

Carers UK   www.carersuk.org
Government website   www.carers.gov.uk
Princess Royal Trust for Carers   www.carers.org
Carersnet   www.carersnet.org.uk
Self-help in Scotland   www.needs-scotland.org

Information and Evidence

NICE eating disorder guidelines   www.nice.org.uk
Scottish guidelines   www.nhshealthquality.org/nhsqis/
                                   CCC_FirstPage.jsp
National Library for Health   www.library.nhs.uk
Clinical Evidence   www.cks.library.nhs.uk

Self-help Organisations

beat
Wensum House
103 Prince of Wales Road
Norwich NR1 1DW
Tel: 0845 634 1414
email: help@b-eat.co.uk; website: www.b-eat.co.uk

North East Eating Disorder Support (NEEDS) Scotland
Eating Disorder Service
Macrobin Centre
Royal Cornhill Hospital
Aberdeen AB25 2ZH
website: www.needs-scotland.org

National Eating Disorders Association
603 Stewart St., Suite 803, Seattle, WA 98101
Business Office: (206) 382–3587
Toll-free Information and Referral Helpline: (800) 931–2237
email: info@NationalEatingDisorders.org
website: www.nationaleatingdisorders.org

1

Shifting responsibility – the lived experience of an eating disorder

Why Read On?

You may have been handed this book by your family or a friend; page open, on this chapter. Or, you may have found this book for yourself or have followed a recommendation. Whatever has brought you here, immaterial of your present circumstances, and however long or short your journey so far, your feelings are mixed but personal to you; *hoping* that someone will recognise, open their eyes, to your plight; *dismayed* and *angered* that others believe you are ill; *captivated* by your secret, your crutch to life and your 'successful' coping tool; *terrified* of your behaviour and *shameful* of its consequences and impact on others. Whoever you are, whatever you feel and no matter how strong, ambivalent or indeed irresolute your desire to change is, you must *trust*. Trust that at some point, somewhere and somehow, you will *need* someone. YOU have to want to get through this but, however much of a self-sufficient island and free agent you profess to be, remember that '*you alone can do it, but you can't do it alone*'.

This book aims to enlighten a carer(s) or those closest to you, maybe a husband, a friend, a mother or a sibling, as to how to guide and support you through your eating disorder. The techniques and information contained here have been built on over time and gleaned from three perspectives – knowledgeable professional, practised carer and recovering sufferer.

There is nothing stopping you from reading this book and also becoming your own carer. Or you can show the book to your friends or therapist and work with it this way.

First, it may be helpful to summarise the topics covered here briefly so you understand the approach your carer may choose to take. Additionally, you may begin to appreciate how having an informed and skilled carer may help you to start your journey. We find that once carers recognise how hard it is to change their own behaviour, they have sympathy for your struggles.

A Snapshot

(1) Animal Metaphors

Eating disorder symptoms have a profound impact on those close to you as well as you, the sufferer. Your behaviour may prompt a whole host of reactions – anger, frustration, despair, tears, panic, anxiety or even ignorance. In Chapter 4 we ask carers to identify and acknowledge how they respond to eating disorder symptoms; do they smother you with protection, safeguarding your every movement? Do they treat you as an invalid or an incapable child, unable to make decisions for yourself? In other words, are they like a *Kangaroo* – with you sheltered and hidden in a pouch. Or, do they charge in with anger and irritation? Do they not understand why you behave as you do: 'just eat more, there, simple' or 'stop visiting the bathroom after meals; problem solved'. In other words, are they like a *Rhino*, with rage and control being the only two solutions they have.

You may find that your carer chooses to ignore your deteriorating health, damaging habits and self-destructive nature. Might it be too painful, too frightening or too real for them to watch? Do they bury their head in the sand, hoping for the best and for time to pass, like an *Ostrich*? Or perhaps they are reduced to tears by your behaviour? – touchy and emotionally unstable, like a *Jellyfish*, carrying both immense guilt and shame for the conviction that they are to blame for 'all of this'. We explain, Chapter 9, that these reactions, although natural and instinctive, are universally unhelpful: both to you and to them, to the rest of the family, and, to your eating disorder. We aim to provide carers with the tools, skills and knowledge to change their response; to work with you rather than against you; to hasten recovery, life and health rather than protract illness, demise and ruin; and, to challenge and weaken your eating disorder rather than strengthen and reinforce it.

(2) The Facts

Chapters 2, 3 and 6 aim to educate carers about eating disorders – improving their ability to recognise symptoms (Chapter 2), dispelling common myths and beliefs (Chapter 3) and acknowledging the potential medical risk and health consequences involved (Chapter 6). It may also be useful for you to have a read of these chapters. You will realise just how unaware and blind the general population is to disordered eating and, importantly, the potential risks and consequences to health, and life, your illness presents for you. Additionally, by sharing common beliefs, you and your carer are both working *together* from a joint perspective, the principle of which can never be underestimated.

(3) Change

Chapter 7 outlines the different stages of change recognised in sufferers. Perhaps you can identify with the text and the diagram on p. 51? A carer needs to appreciate that **you** have to want to change – only you can make the decision that you want life, health and a future. Remember, *'you alone can do it'*. No amount of bullying, coercion, deception or force can sway you if you are determined to stick with the illness. However, from Chapter 7, a carer learns that they have a role in the process of change; giving you time, opportunity and encouragement to express the pros and the cons of changing. You need this. Remember that, *'you can't do it alone'*. Furthermore, using the 'Readiness Ruler' described in the chapter gives you a useful concrete marker and score of your progress.

(4) Communication

Communication – an essential part in the process to recovery – is the focus of Chapter 8. Maybe you feel that no one listens to you? Maybe other people in the house just don't 'get you'? Maybe no one recognises how hard you struggle or comments when you do succeed and achieve? Good communication is hard to perfect, especially when a pattern of strained relationships and resentment has developed in a household. Chapter 8, through sequential Communication Skills topics, gives a carer the resources to steer you towards health in the long term and, in the short term, improve home life, atmosphere and family relationships.

(5) Lost Emotions

You may be oblivious to the emotional underpinnings of your eating disorder – is it 'just' about weight, 'just' about calories, exercise and what you see when you look in the mirror? Or, are you acutely aware of how your eating disorder dulls, 'takes the edge off' and controls strong emotions and intense feelings? Whatever your present stance, take a moment to read the following. The sufferer below writes of her relationship with her anorexia nervosa, aptly named by her as 'Ed', on entering inpatient treatment:

> Nurses put up with my outbursts, my anger, my tears, my frustration and my screams as two years of repressed feelings and emotions poured out uncontrollably. They let me fight, they let me cry and they let me grieve for the loss of my so-called 'friend'. Ed squashes all emotions – good and bad. With Ed, there is no anger, no laughter, no rage, no joy, no sadness, no pleasure, no anxiety,

no pain, just numbness. No feelings at all, nothing. Ed is a barrier and a protector. With Ed, you feel untouchable, invisible and immune. Gradually, after weeks of treatment my feelings started to flow – so intense and unmanageable at first. My emotions were extreme, frightening, unknown and so quick to change. Calmness could evolve into terror, laughter into shame within moments. Tears rolled down my face at every opportunity. The more I engage with life, the more I learn about how to manage these alien feelings. The numbness that Ed creates blocks out everything. With an Eating Disorder, a sufferer misses out on all the amazing emotions that life brings, just so that they can escape the painful emotions. Treatment teaches a sufferer the tools they need to tackle life along with its resulting emotions.

Other eating behaviours such as bingeing, over-exercising and vomiting may also be a way of trying to soothe or distract from intense feelings. Or, maybe you feel constantly physically 'full'; enormous, like a balloon, taut and stretched, and unable to fill yourself up anymore? Try and reconsider this. Perhaps you are full of suppressed and unvented feelings and emotions? Maybe you relieve this 'fullness' by restricting what you eat or perhaps you purge or vomit?

Chapter 10 coaches a carer on how to be 'emotionally intelligent'; an important skill to grasp. Maybe no one has ever asked how you feel before? Maybe talking about feelings in your house is taboo? Maybe you can't recognise or identify your emotions? The best way to learn is often by example and Chapter 10 explains to a carer the importance of discussing emotions in recovery.

(6) Eating and Behaviour

Chapters 11 and 12 deal with aspects of eating (under and over) and Chapter 13 with other additional problem behaviours. Maybe you have strict rules regarding food? For example, 'to be eaten, food has to be earned, deserved and worked hard for' or 'food must be kept separate; no mixing of proteins, carbohydrates or vegetables'. You might be able to identify with some of the rules on pp. 125–126? Maybe you have behaviours that keep you 'safe' after eating, such as exercising, vomiting or using laxatives? To break free from your eating disorder, you also need to break free from such behaviours and rules. Chapter 11 explains how a carer can help you obtain distance and separation from these rules; through conversation and weighing up the pros and cons (p. 136); through 'naming and shaming' your personal rules (p. 150) and by using an ABC approach (p. 142). Furthermore, however resistant you may be to change or to help, practical suggestions of how a carer is to assist you best at mealtimes and with food are described. *'You can't do it alone'* is particularly apt in terms of eating. Chapter 12 explains how a pattern of food addiction can be built up so that you are beset by intense cravings, it also describes how changes in the environment can help a dysregulated appetite system.

There may be aspects of your behaviour which other people in the house find difficult to cope with – e.g. vomiting, isolating, bingeing. There may also be aspects of behaviour which you, yourself, find tough or tiring to cope with – e.g. cleaning rituals, cooking rituals, constant negative self-ruminations. Perhaps you are ready or willing to change certain behaviours but more reluctant to alter those which provide you with the greatest degree of 'safety'? In Chapter 13, a carer can learn techniques for guiding and supporting you through the process of relinquishing problem behaviours. Distraction activities, challenging your beliefs through discussion and, again, the fundamental psychological ABC approach, are all key tools.

Collected Thoughts

What has been the response from sufferers whose carers have undertaken this approach?

- **Reassurance**: 'I felt they (my parents) became "lighter" and "freer" somehow. It gave them comfort that other people face the same issues, the same problems and same challenges. They were then less stressed around me.'

- **Solving isolation:** 'It was like, for years, they (my parents) were just trapped with me in my illness. They wouldn't leave me on my own, wouldn't go on holiday, out to the cinema or anywhere. The whole family just lived through and focused on my eating disorder. It was like we were all trapped in a bubble. The book, I think, gave them scope to look outside the illness in addition to caring; to take time just for them, to do things they enjoyed and to live their lives, instead of living everything through me and my illness.'

- **Revealed secrets:** 'Up until my Mum began to learn more about eating disorders, mine was a secret. It was private and just for me. I was devious and, wow, I was good at it! Somehow, her knowledge "exposed" my illness. She'd read the tricks and she knew my deceptive ways. The illness became not so individual and not so personal. Somehow a barrier was broken down. I was furious to begin with but, in retrospect, it was the only way for me to start the recovery process.'

- **Understanding:** 'What's in your head is really complex for others to understand. They just don't get the fear, the guilt, the self-repulsion. It's all so inconceivable. They (my parents) weren't aware of the feelings behind my illness. For them, initially it was about the food – about getting me to eat more or keeping as much down me as possible. They started to realise, after reading, that it was so much more than this – sensitivity, repressed feelings, personality types, self-esteem, interpreting social interactions, etc. Their response to me changed totally.'

- **Whose decision is it anyway?:** 'I think my Mum realised that if my life was going to change, I had to want it to. She left more decisions up to me and gave me extra responsibilities. It was hard not to abuse her trust at times but the guilt and sense of shame I had if I did, was unbearable. I think if she hadn't have "taken a back seat" then I would just have stayed stuck for years.'

- **Reality check:** 'By this stage I'd decided that I wanted to change.

I'd discussed the pros and the cons of my illness with my parents so many times. I knew them all so well! The frustrating thing was that whenever food was involved, my world narrowed. I just couldn't see that I had future plans, hopes and aspirations. All I could see was what was on the plate in front of me. They reminded me of the "real world" and the "bigger picture" at mealtimes. It got me through.'

ACTION POINTS ➤

- If you have the courage to read this book you will have taken the first step to being able to see beyond your eating disorder to the bigger life that will be in store for you without it.

- You will be able to gain a new perspective – what it might be like for others looking on.

- Being able to take an overview about your own and others' thinking, emotions, sensations, memories and perceptions is a large leap to mature wisdom.

◀ REFLECTION POINTS

1. 'You alone can do it, but you can't do it alone' – in this book we try to share with carers some of the understanding that can help them feel less perplexed by this illness and more able to cope.

2. Secrets either within or without yourself are not helpful. Openness and respect are key components for recovery. This book lays open some of the confusion about eating disorders.

skills-based learning for caring for a loved one

2

Caring for a loved one with an eating disorder – first steps

The persistent extreme behaviours associated with eating disorders are frightening and confusing when you first encounter them. You may fear that your loved one has cancer when you see the extreme weight loss. Similarly, persistent vomiting is upsetting. Many facets of the problem are held in secret. You may have no real idea what is going on, but your instincts tell you that it is something terrible, with potentially long-term consequences. Recognising that the problem is an eating disorder may be hard for you and even for your general practitioner. Where can you start? The following section may help.

1. Is This an Eating Disorder?

With so many people on a diet, how do you know it is not just a passing phase? In Table 2.1, below, there are some pointers that can alert you to the fact that something more serious than dieting is involved. Someone developing an eating disorder may have several of the signs shown in Table 2.1.

2. Broaching the Subject – Acceptance

The next step is to get the individual concerned willing to accept that there may be a problem.

TABLE 2.1 Distinguishing Normal Dieting from Eating Disorder Symptoms

- Denial of diet – dieters talk about it all the time
- Change in food rules, e.g. becoming vegetarian
- Denial of hunger and craving
- Covering up the weight loss, possibly by wearing baggy clothes
- Increased interest in food – cooking for others, scouring recipe books, supermarket shelf gazing and calorie counting
- Claims of needing to eat less than others or only very small portions
- Eating slowly, with small mouthfuls
- Avoiding eating with others, e.g. the excuse of having eaten already or eaten elsewhere
- Behaviour becoming more compulsive and ritualised – cleaning, tidying, organising, washing, etc.
- Becoming socially isolated and low in mood
- Frequently disappearing to the bathroom – during meals and after. The smell of vomit or excessive use of air fresheners about the house
- A new or increased exercise routine – strict, rigid and gruelling.

People with eating disorders are not easy to help. As an observer you may notice that eating behaviours (either too much or too little) are impacting not only on the quality of life of your loved one but on your life too. However, you may find it impossible to raise your concerns effectively as they get brushed aside. One of the core clinical signs of an eating disorder is that the individual perceives some positive benefit to their condition – a sense of well-being, power, control, uniqueness, etc.

Some individuals persist with their meagre dietary rations. For others, the compulsion to eat breaks their resolve. They then feel driven to use extreme measures to compensate for their 'indulgence' with over-exercise, vomiting or laxatives. A pattern rather like an addiction can slowly develop with the individual fasting or subsisting on a monotonous low-calorie diet for long periods;

skills-based learning for caring for a loved one

then, suddenly, if a small portion of palatable food passes their lips, being unable to stop eating. Other compulsive, driven behaviours such as over-exercise or quirky rituals can occur. Understanding change, and how carers can encourage moving away from behaviour with negative consequences, is further discussed in Chapter 7.

You may feel frozen and powerless as your loved one becomes angry and/or humiliated when you broach the subject. With eating a core aspect of life, relationships can become fraught both in families and in professional settings. Chapter 4 describes the common reactions to Edi. Chapter 9 explains how to tackle strains in relationships.

3. Broaching the Subject – Preparation

It can help to prepare yourself and even practise for the possible scenarios that might arise when you broach the subject with Edi. Decide where and when you will introduce the conversation – a quiet room with no danger of interruption or distraction is best.

In this preparatory phase it can help to make notes of the possible symptoms and behaviours that have made you feel uneasy. Have these observations to hand.

Find as much information about eating disorders as you can – websites and helpline numbers are given in the Preface – and compare your observations with case descriptions. Talk about your concerns with a wise friend.

It takes time for the individual concerned to be able to step aside from the compulsive spirals of thought and action and be willing or able to listen to your point of view. You need to help the individual shift their focus from their increasingly narrowed eating/food-driven perspective onto deeper values such as their health and lifetime ambitions.

Be wary of joining in, and hence encouraging, 'eating disorder talk' such as discussion about food, calories, body shape or weight. These are major preoccupations for the individual – they have infinite and detailed knowledge of these topics and are well practised in raising them in conversation. Stepping away from this 'dance' will require you to be reflective and self-disciplined. Getting into an argument will make things worse so, if necessary, agree to disagree and, by doing so, keep the bridges of communication open for later work. For the interim, watchful waiting is the key.

Some general preparatory advice is given in Table 2.2 below.

TABLE 2.2 How to Broach the Subject

- If you are suspicious, *act* – ask *gentle* questions, *calmly* express your concern, talk of your observations
- Remember – people with eating disorders reject the idea that they have a problem
- Do not be shy, dismiss or ignore symptoms or give up on the person
- Let them know that you know they have a problem. It may be a long while before they themselves can confront and admit that they have a problem
- Choose the moment carefully – a relaxed atmosphere is best, away from mealtimes
- Do not go for browbeating – you do not need to win each battle
- Be prepared for setbacks, especially initially.

4. Broaching the Subject – Scripting

Try and script a possible interaction. Think carefully of what you want to say about your concerns and imagine Edi's response. As in all things, practice is invaluable, perhaps with another family member or a friend.

Try to position yourself as a slightly detached observer, a fly on the wall:

'I have noticed . . . I am concerned about . . . Please can you talk to me about it . . .'

Be calm and compassionate. Talk and act as if the individual has mixed feelings about change, as if there are two parts to them; the 'well side' and the 'ill side'.

The following are some starters to help carers develop their own useful phrases. More are offered throughout the book:

TABLE 2.3   Developing Useful Phrases

- Normalise mixed feelings:
  'Part of you feels . . ., yet part of you wants to . . .'
  See Chapter 7 about ambivalence re change.

- Describe the facts as you see them calmly and with warmth:
  'I see you think . . . I think you feel . . . I noticed that . . . How can I help?'

- Listen carefully to the answers:
  'Sounds like this might be the way you see things . . .? Have I got that right?'
  Use reflective listening and affirmation to build trust (Chapter 8).

- Find out what if anything concerns the person with an eating disorder:
  'The doctor says it would be better to reduce exercising because your BMI is very low. What do you think would have to happen for you to do this?'
  The motivational 'Readiness Ruler' (Chapter 7, 'Understanding Change') is a useful tool.

- Listen without judgement:
  'Everyone has different views. This is not the way I see things; I accept you feel differently.'

- Modulate your emotional reaction, remain *calm and compassionate* (Chapter 10).

- Ask what you and others might be able to do to help:
  'Is there anything I can do to help?'

- Genuine support, love, kindness and respect can make a difference.

- Express all positive thoughts and comments as often as possible:
  'Thanks for . . . I like it when . . .'

- Phrase comments on negative eating disorder behaviours in non-judgemental tones; sandwich such comments between reassurances that it is the behaviour you dislike, you still love the person:
  'I don't like it when you shout at me; I love you – and still don't like it when you shout at me. I love you and am concerned about you; I don't like it when . . .'

- Be patient – it is difficult to change.

---

5. If You Fail this Time

> *'I can't get through to her. She denies everything.'*
>
> *'She just got so angry, saying I was being overprotective and imagining things.'*
>
> *'She said that she was just having to work hard for exams. She said she was fine though.'*
>
> *'Somehow we ended up talking about me! That really wasn't the point!'*

Don't be despondent if your first, and maybe many more subsequent attempts, are met with anger, are ridiculed, ignored, denied or brushed aside. Don't give up and keep watching. Wait for other opportunities and don't leave. Edi needs you but is not at the stage to realise it themselves.

6. Other Support?

This early stage is very difficult. You may feel lost, alone and confused. You may not be able to get to the stage when your loved one agrees that he or she wants help but you could do more preparatory work. For example, you could go to your general practitioner yourself, describe what you observe – notes of incidents and frequency of behaviour can be useful here – and ask what help and resources would be available in your local area if and when your loved one decides to go for help.

skills-based learning for caring for a loved one

ACTION POINTS ➤

- Doctors have concerns about confidentiality. Therefore they are unable to give you individualised information but they are able to describe the problem in general.

- Eating disorders are relatively rare; it may not be an area your GP knows a lot about.

- If you find yourself getting frequent negative feelings towards your loved one, seek support. *beat* runs an eating disorders helpline. It may be worth speaking to someone who has experience and can empathise.

⬅ REFLECTION POINTS

1. Is this an Eating Disorder? – WATCH for SIGNS.

2. REMEMBER: Getting an individual to ACCEPT they have a problem is key but NEVER easy.

3. PREPARE yourself to broach the subject. Gather information, research and talk to others if possible. Decide on a time and place.

4. SCRIPT in your head. Rehearse the conversation.

5. DON'T GIVE UP. Your concern may initially fall on deaf ears.

6. Seek SUPPORT. You don't have to survive this alone.

Additional Resources

There is additional material that may help carers at this stage on our website www.eatingresearch.com (Crane, 2006), and also materials for the sufferer. *Anorexia and bulimia in the family* (Smith, 2004) may also help.

beat Helpline: 0845 634 1414.

Further Reading

Crane, A. *How to recognise an eating disorder*. www.eatingresearch.com, 2006.
Smith, G. *Anorexia and bulimia in the family*. Chichester, UK: Wiley, 2004.

3

Working with a joint understanding of the illness – basic facts about eating disorders

The five most common questions about *any* illness are:

1. What are the symptoms?

2. What are the causes?

3. What is the expected time course?

4. What are the consequences (a) for the sufferer (b) for close others?

5. How controllable/treatable is it?

Although general 'eating disorder information' is applicable to most sufferers, there are also unique aspects to every case. Mistaken assumptions about the illness can lead to unhelpful coping strategies. This in turn will cause distress, not just to the sufferer, but also to family and friends.

In the following section we give just a few examples of some common mistaken assumptions. You probably have your own beliefs – which may, or may not, be helpful in coping with the illness.

Common Myths about Eating Disorders

- 'Families (in particular mothers) are responsible for their daughter/son developing an eating disorder.'

- 'People with eating disorders choose to have their illness. They want to be ill/to die/or to not grow up.'

- 'People with eating disorders are trying to punish their parents, or whoever they live with.'

- 'Families with an eating disorder in their midst need therapy.'

- 'Eating disorders are all to do with vanity and aspirations to be a model.'

- 'It's just another form of teenage attention-seeking behaviour and rebellion.'

- 'It's something that people grow out of, a passing phase.'

- 'The person is cured, completely, after a period of inpatient treatment.'

- 'You must do all you can to please and humour the invalid.'

- 'The hospital and treatment team can always cure them.'

- 'It is just a question of eating.'

When family members or anyone else hold beliefs like these, stress is increased as negative emotions such as guilt, remorse, anger, frustration and recrimination flourish. To date, evidence for the causes of eating disorders is patchy, with much scientific research still focused on the area. Many written sources contain myths about the illness which can be hurtful and unhelpful.

What is known is that an eating disorder is not just a problem with eating and food. There are deeper issues relating to identity, emotions, beliefs and values. Treatment can take time, but some aspects of recovery take place within the context of normal development.

It is helpful if everyone, sufferer, family members and health professionals, all share a common understanding of anorexia nervosa and bulimia nervosa. Important knowledge, beliefs and attitudes are best shared. In an ideal situation, everyone would be working from the same understanding, with information based on research evidence. Not easy to achieve in practice. However, the following is a start.

Facts So Far . . .

There is great uncertainty about what causes an eating disorder. There does not seem to be any one clear cause.

Recent research into biological processes suggests that many of the mechanisms that underlie eating disorders are not under conscious or wilful control. Rather, a network of biological systems such as the processing of information, emotions and organisation of behaviour contribute to the illness. Some of these are fixed and are part of the genetic makeup, whereas others emerge from environmental events and upbringing.

Often, though not always, an eating disorder develops at or around puberty. A key aspect in this situation may be the critical timing of the illness during a phase of complex brain maturation/development. A self-perpetuating trap is triggered as starvation and learned behaviours interrupt this developmental process, making recovery more difficult.

Within the population, genetic factors account for over 50 per cent of the risk.[1] The mechanisms connecting genes and behaviour are unknown at the present time. However, both emotional and thinking dispositions appear to be of relevance in eating disorders. For example, people with eating disorders are more sensitive to perceived signals of threat, and appear to be less adept in their use of emotional intelligence. These characteristics may be innate, or may develop as part of the illness process.

A thinking style that increases illness risk is one that favours attention to detail with a superior ability to focus – but at the expense of flexibility.[2,3] Being able to concentrate and focus on detail can be a great asset – unless the focus becomes so intense that the bigger picture is lost, for example when Edi focuses on food and eating to the exclusion of everything else (e.g. school/work/friends/social activities, etc.) including health.

The response of the brain to food-related cues is unusual in people with eating disorders[4,5] in that the front of the brain, involved in decision making and emotional regulation, also becomes activated. It is as though the meaning and reaction to food becomes entangled with brain processes regulating motivation and planning. When people who have recovered from an eating disorder are shown images of food, the same brain areas remain abnormally activated but several new regions in the frontal part of the brain become activated too. One suggestion is that during the recovery process, new networks are recruited to compensate for the persistent overactivity in the key frontal areas. Furthermore, people with eating disorders have been found to have a chemical imbalance in their brain. Receptors for serotonin and dopamine – both key signalling chemicals in the frontal part of the brain – are reduced in both the acute state of illness and after recovery.[6]

TABLE 3.1 What Can We Learn from This?

- These findings argue against the myth that eating disorders are caused by wilful stubbornness on the part of the sufferer.

- Individuals with eating disorders are not on a hunger strike. They are not trying to do something to anyone else. Rather, the symptoms are a marker of deeper levels of stress and distress which leave their imprint on brain function.

- The longer starvation continues, the more difficult it is to recover as the brain remains immature.

- The brain is a 'plastic' organ, i.e. it can grow and respond to environmental events. Stress and starvation can inhibit this process.

- In order to promote recovery, individuals with an eating disorder need to learn to practise behaving differently or even to oppose their natural instincts. This process will help form and 'tone up' new brain pathways.

How Are Eating Disorders Treated?

As yet there is little evidence to support any one form of treatment in eating disorders, but forms of psychotherapy – talking treatments – are found to be the most successful and acceptable. These need to be combined with careful physical monitoring. In some cases, these treatments and monitoring may be effective through outpatient departments. In other cases, nutritional support is necessary in a specialised hospital unit. Inpatient treatment is usually successful in terms of weight gain in the short term but, if the individual groundwork in addressing the underlying emotional problems is not done, there is a high chance of relapse.

A first-stage treatment target is often whether or not nutritional health can be restored. The medical consequences of starvation, such as the failure of bone development and reproductive function, are reversed by weight gain. Likewise, salt imbalances from laxative overuse and/or vomiting, are reversed during a period of remission. The brain control of appetite is the primary problem and should be the focus of treatment (see Chapter 12 for more details). However, it should be noted that brain development gets interrupted by starvation and so people can be stuck if they remain undernourished for long periods.

Once weight gain has been achieved, a secondary target is weight maintenance. Can the individual sustain their weight without a high level of external control (e.g. what happens between outpatient treatment appointments, or on weekend leave from hospital care)?

How Long Will It Last?

The course of an eating disorder is variable. Results from specialist centres suggest that on average the duration is 5–6 years. Thus, if an eating disorder starts in adolescence most people continue to have problems when they are young adults. However, within this average envelope there are people who recover within a year and those who have an enduring severe course of illness.

We have developed simple assessment forms, which can be used to make an estimate of the severity and long-term course of the illness – see www.eatingresearch.com in the section for professionals. These forms were designed for use after a period of treatment (the response to treatment is an important marker of prognosis).

TABLE 3.2 Factors Associated with a More Protracted Illness

- A long duration of illness
- Severity of weight loss
- Vomiting and purging
- Additional psychological problems, e.g. obsessive compulsive disorder
- Difficulty gaining weight within treatment
- Inability to restore weight in the normal range, i.e. BMI (19–24) for adults with inpatient treatment
- Factors within the family leading to high stress levels.

What Is the Prognosis?

As the course of an eating disorder is variable between individuals, so is its prognosis. Some useful points to remember are that:

- The outcome of younger cases, or those with a short duration of illness, is good.

- Effective treatment *early* in the course of the illness, which is less than three years, leads to a good outcome in 90 per cent of cases.

- And, restoring weight to a normal level in hospital, by itself, does not ensure that the outcome is good. Understanding and unpicking the association of food and weight issues with emotions, styles of thinking and relationships is essential for effective treatment.

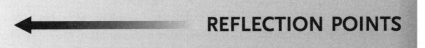

REFLECTION POINTS

1. Myths are unhelpful and hurtful. They impact on attitudes and behaviours towards you, other family members and Edi, as well as increasing stress levels.

2. Whilst there is uncertainty about the causes of eating disorders, the consequences are clear. Professionals and family members can modify the consequences by working to decrease the time spent in a severely emaciated state and coaching the individual to attain mature emotional, cognitive and social development.

3. The development of an eating disorder is NOT under conscious or wilful control.

ACTION POINT

Dispel your own myths and beliefs about eating disorders by using the information sources listed in the Preface. Share the information with family and friends involved in Edi's care. Try to ensure that everyone is working from the same understanding.

Reference List

1. Bulik, C.M., Sullivan, P.F., Wade, T.D., Kendler, K.S. Twin studies of eating disorders: a review. *International Journal of Eating Disorders* (2000), **27**:1–20.
2. Tchanturia, K., Anderluh, M.B., Morris, R.G., Rabe-Hesketh, S., Collier, D.A.,

Sanchez, P. *et al.* Cognitive flexibility in eating disorder and bulimia nervosa. *Journal of the International Neuropsychological Society* (2004), **10**:513–20.

3. Tchanturia, K., Morris, R.G., Anderluh, M.B., Collier, D.A., Nikolaou, V., Treasure, J. Set shifting in anorexia nervosa: an examination before and after weight gain, in full recovery and relationship to childhood and adult OCPD traits. *Journal of Psychiatric Research* (2004), **38**:545–52.

4. Uher, R., Murphy, T., Brammer, M.J., Dalgleish, T., Phillips, M.L., Ng, V.W. *et al.* Medial prefrontal cortex activity associated with symptom provocation in eating disorders. *American Journal of Psychiatry* (2004), **161**:1238–46.

5. Uher, R., Brammer, M.J., Murphy, T., Campbell, I.C., Ng, V.W., Williams, S.C. *et al.* Recovery and chronicity in anorexia nervosa: brain activity associated with differential outcomes. *Biological Psychiatry* (2003), **54**:934–42.

6. Frank, G.K., Kaye, W.H., Meltzer, C.C., Price, J.C., Greer, P., McConaha, C. *et al.* Reduced 5-HT2A receptor binding after recovery from anorexia nervosa. *Biological Psychiatry* (2002), **52**:896–906.

Further Reading

Miller, W., Rollnick, S. *Motivational interviewing: Preparing people to change addictive behaviour*. New York: Guilford, 1991.

Miller, W., Rollnick, S. *Motivational interviewing*. New York: The Guilford Press, 2002.

Treasure, J. *Anorexia nervosa: A survival guide for sufferers and those caring for someone with an eating disorder*. Hove, East Sussex: Psychology Press, 1997.

Venables, J.F. *Guy's Hospital Report 80*, 213–22214. 1–1–1930.

4

Which kind of carer are you?

As food plays a key role in life and social interactions, eating disorders impact on relationships. In our experience, the responses by carers, described below, are NATURAL and TYPICAL reactions to eating disorder symptoms. These are INSTINCTIVE reactions in a concerned and frightened carer but RECOGNISING yourself in the animal metaphors depicted may ultimately improve your rapport and connection with Edi. Chapter 9 goes on to explain how to put these traits to a more productive and beneficial use.

How Do You React? Behaviour

Animal metaphors are used below to illustrate common BEHAVIOURS that carers may get drawn into while playing out in reaction to eating disorder symptoms.

Kangaroo Care

'Kangaroo Care' reaction emerges when Edi's fragile physical state draws you in to protect him or her completely, to keep them safe, as if in a pouch. In the case of anorexia, the overt effects of starvation speak volumes whereas, although bulimia may not be as noticeable to the outside world, and the individual appears

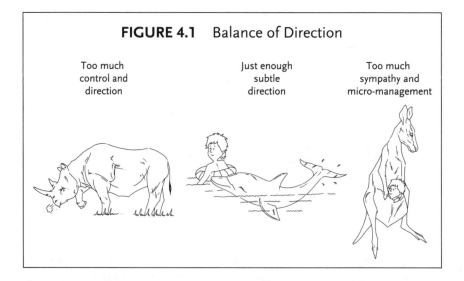

FIGURE 4.1 Balance of Direction

Too much control and direction

Just enough subtle direction

Too much sympathy and micro-management

'well', family and friends soon become aware of illness-related behaviours and overprotection ensues. Kangaroo will do everything possible to support and protect, taking over all sorts of aspects of life in an attempt to help. Kangaroo will treat Edi with kid gloves in an effort to try to avoid causing any possible upset or stress. Kangaroo will accommodate to all demands, whether they are rational or driven by the eating disorder. In bulimia for instance, Kangaroo might accept having to shop for much larger amounts than formerly, or having to replace missing food; in anorexia, Kangaroo might drive miles to find a special food which just *might* tempt Edi's appetite . . . *The downside of taking over all Edi's responsibilities is that Edi will fail to learn how to approach and master the challenges of life, and become trapped in the role of an infant.*

The Rhinoceros Response

As carers you become stressed and exhausted by Edi's seemingly unremitting intransigence in the face of the apparently, simple solution – to eat a nutritious and adequate amount to preserve Edi's health – and you may get drawn into adopting 'Rhinoceros Response' (see Figure 4.1 above). Or your temperament may be one that focuses on detail and so you want Edi to understand your analysis of the situation. Tempers may additionally become short as food disappears, the bathroom is in constant use, sinks and toilets are blocked or family meals are continually interrupted. Rhino attempts to persuade and convince Edi to change by argument, as if charging at and trying to smash with logic the eating disordered behaviour and beliefs. *The downside of this is that if Edi obeys, confidence in the belief that Edi can do this without assistance will not be developed. Or, as is more likely, Edi may spend all energies in self-protection, arguing back with eating disorder logic, rehearsing all the distorted eating disordered thinking – and digging a deeper hole to hide in.*

The Dolphin

The image in the middle, of the figure wearing a life vest, represents Edi. It is as if they are at sea, with the eating disorder as their life belt. They will be unwilling to give up the perceived safety of the life belt whilst they feel that the world is stressful and dangerous. Continuing the animal metaphor we suggest that rather than falling into Rhinoceros or Kangaroo extremes, try to model yourself on a dolphin, nudging Edi into safety. Dolphin may at times swim ahead, leading the way and guiding the passage, at other times swim alongside coaching and giving encouragement, and at times when Edi is making positive progress quietly swim behind.

How Do You React? Emotion

The other dimension of the relationship which can be difficult to get right is the EMOTIONAL response. Again, animal metaphors are used to describe what happens.

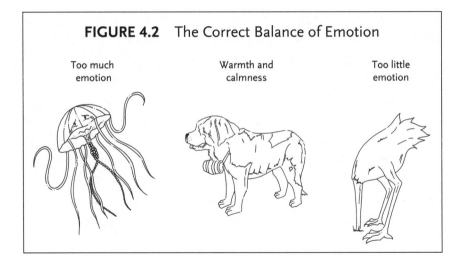

FIGURE 4.2 The Correct Balance of Emotion

Too much emotion

Warmth and calmness

Too little emotion

The Ostrich

Some family members may find it difficult to cope with the distress and upset of challenging or confronting eating disorder behaviours. They try to avoid thinking or talking about the problems at all – the 'Ostrich Approach', with head firmly in the sand! While trying to ignore, and not admitting to the effects of Edi's behaviour, Ostrich may – or may not – be well aware of consequences for the family. Ostrich may spend as much time away from the home situation as possible, working or finding any other activity rather than confronting the difficult situation and behaviour of Edi.

The Jellyfish

Sometimes people can be engulfed in an intense and transparent emotional response, perhaps because they hold some false interpretations of the illness (see Chapter 3 for myths and beliefs). They may hold the belief that this illness means they have failed as a parent. High levels of self-blame produce a 'Jellyfish Response'. Alternatively you may be a perfectionist in terms of your parenting skills and expectations and hold yourself totally responsible for

skills-based learning for caring for a loved one

your child's life and happiness. This sensitive, often tearful, Jelly-fish reaction may additionally be due to exhaustion and despair. When carers feel helpless and have this reaction, their own health is affected. Comfort, advice and support may be needed to prevent depression and a further deterioration in the situation.

The St Bernard Dog

Or, as a carer, are you like the image in the middle – a St Bernard? A St Bernard responds consistently – unfailing, reliable and dependable in all circumstances. A St Bernard is calm and collected – even when situations are dangerous. He does not panic or shout and scream, which may cause an avalanche. He is organised, and provides companionship, warmth and nurture. He is dedicated to the welfare and safety of those who are helplessly lost. Calm, warm, nurturing – try and model yourself on a St Bernard.

←———————— **REFLECTION POINTS**

Think who depicts YOUR BEHAVIOUR?

1. Kangaroo – overprotective, too accommodating and too controlling

2. Rhinoceros – angry and stampeding

3. Dolphin – guiding, coaching, encouraging and subtle

Think who depicts YOUR EMOTIONS?

1. Ostrich – preferring escapism and avoidance

2. Jellyfish – too emotional and sensitive

3. St Bernard – calm, warm and nurturing

5

Stress, strain and developing resilience

Stress: Why Are Carers Susceptible?

A mild degree of stress can serve as a challenge. This can be energising and fulfilling if we can eventually master the problem. However, unrelenting stress, with which it is beyond our capacity to cope, turns into strain and leads to distress. Living with an eating disorder is a huge challenge, even to a large team of highly trained professionals, let alone any individual family.

One of the difficulties is that the problem is multifaceted and impinges on all areas of family life. Figure 5.1 illustrates some of the problem areas to be faced, based upon research and clinical work we have done involving carers.

When the strength of the eating disorder is high, there is a danger that a family's resilience will fail. Once there is a collapse of coping resources, family members can become depressed or overanxious, or walk away from the problems, all of which will impact on Edi and their care. Tension between being drawn in to protect and try to help Edi, and the resulting rejection (both active and passive) of that help lead to further misery.

Coping and resilience can be improved through getting the right information at the right time, by learning new skills and building on existing ones. This applies to anyone in close proximity to the sufferer, whether family or friend. The closeness of the relationship and amount of time spent together are major factors in how draining on resources the experience can be. In specialist

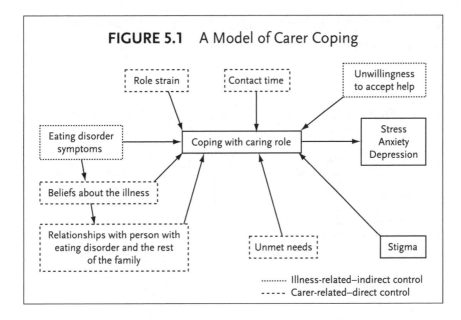

FIGURE 5.1 A Model of Carer Coping

Role strain

Contact time

Unwillingness to accept help

Eating disorder symptoms

Coping with caring role

Stress
Anxiety
Depression

Beliefs about the illness

Relationships with person with eating disorder and the rest of the family

Unmet needs

Stigma

·········· Illness-related–indirect control
----- Carer-related–direct control

units treating eating disorders, staff burnout, sickness or difficulties with recruitment and staff continuity frequently occur. In families, individual members may become exhausted and isolated and develop clinical levels of depression or anxiety.

ACTION POINT ➤

Look again at Figure 5.1, the model of carer coping.

Consider each of the boxes carefully. Perhaps you can identify which apply to you and your family – for instance, which eating disorder symptoms cause most distress? Does anyone in the family show signs of stress, anxiety or depression? It may be helpful to rank each of the areas in order of difficulty for you so that you can prioritise the chapters.

Using the model outlined in Figure 5.1, Figure 5.2 adds strategies to cope with each of the problem areas.

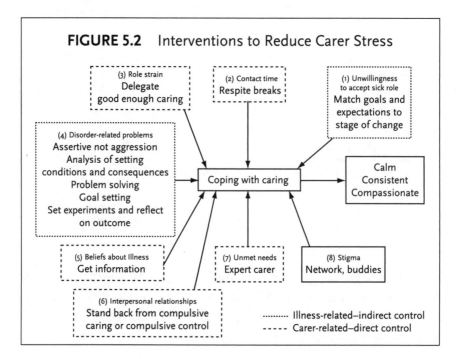

FIGURE 5.2 Interventions to Reduce Carer Stress

The following text gives you more in-depth information about each of these areas; we will go round the model anticlockwise, starting in the top right-hand corner.

1. Unwillingness to Accept Help

If there is a huge divergence between your understanding of the eating disorder and its consequences, and that of Edi's, it can cause much friction. In anorexia, carers see that Edi is ill and physically frail, whereas it is Edi's strongly held belief that his or her current weight and physical state are satisfactory. In Edi's view, nothing is wrong. Sufferers of bulimia are also sceptical of the medical consequences of their behaviour. They may feel incapable or unable to conceive their life without the 'release' or

skills-based learning for caring for a loved one

coping strategy that purging gives them. It is thus very difficult to persuade Edi to seek medical help – and even more difficult for Edi to adhere to any advice given. This is intensely frustrating for all carers, and for professionals. Chapter 7 deals extensively with the prospect of Change.

2. Contact Time

Often families, determined to do their best for Edi, will be totally committed in their efforts to help and try to be with him or her as much as possible. Unfortunately this superhuman effort can be counterproductive as it can lead to a build-up of tension which may explode unexpectedly, or come out in other more subtle ways. Carers have told us that they find that one of the important things in helping their loved one is to start to take some time off; to step back, to reflect and have respite from their caring duties.

Caring for yourself is of vital importance as a core skill in managing eating disorders, enabling you to maintain a calm, compassionate stance. *This is impossible unless you can nurture and replenish yourself.* Not only is this important for your own well-being, but it also models a reasonable level of self-care for the person with an eating disorder.

3. Role Strain – Fostering Consistency at Home with Family and Other Carers

Within families (and also within professional teams) there are often heated differences of opinion and polarised, conflicting strategies about the role and responsibilities that each family member should take in relation to the eating disorder. This inevitably causes conflict and distress and an inconsistent reaction to the illness. *Consistency* is a core skill and so needs special attention. Husbands, siblings, grandparents and other family members may feel neglected and resent – either passively or by active protest – the attention devoted to Edi.

Try not to let concern over the illness take over your life entirely.

Find time and energy for other family members and their activities, and, as emphasised above, for yourself. This is not easy with such a demanding illness, which affects so many aspects of life, and it may be necessary to simplify life in some way, perhaps by asking for help and delegating, or perhaps by finding one role you can drop.

4. Disorder-related Problems

Although meals are the major focus and cause many problems, other symptoms – depression, anxieties, explosive anger, compulsions and rituals, excessive exercise, vomiting, social isolation, to name a few – intrude into family life and are very difficult to manage. It is best if families can work together to plan some time to share and explore ideas and strategies about managing symptoms. Chapters 10, 11 and 12 focus on different approaches to help you, and Edi, problem solve and cope with challenging behaviours.

5. Beliefs about the Illness

In Chapter 3, we discussed some of the common assumptions and myths held about eating disorders. These false beliefs can be harmful as they can trigger emotional responses which can get in the way of being calm, consistent and compassionate, and can fuel some of the less-than-helpful personal interactions.

It is possible to alter how aroused and stressed you are by altering how you think about an event. This is the basis of a very successful form of treatment; cognitive behavioural therapy or CBT. Consider the following example – you cannot get to sleep, you are on holiday in a town where a festival is happening and there is noise outside of people laughing, talking and dancing. If you allow your thoughts to be dominated by the idea that people are being inconsiderate, rude and deliberately trying to upset you, it is likely that you will continue to toss and turn as you become more angry. On the other hand, if you try to take a different perspective – ask yourself whether the intentions of the others are basically on the side of good. Yes, they are enjoying the pleasures of social connection and contributing to fun and happiness. You may now find that your feelings about the noise can change from anger to pleasure and compassion. The sensation of arousal and being wound up also settles and you can relax. This can allow your behaviour to change from lying tired and restless to peaceful sleep.

In the context of caring for someone with an eating disorder, you may have a preconceived idea that their illness is a wilful act of selfish, attention-seeking behaviour. You may begin to resent Edi – they create family arguments, tension and stress and require much attention and nurture. They are stubborn, obstinate, rude, and unpredictable and purposelessly go against all your advice. However, informing yourself of the nature of their illness changes your thinking. You read about the subject and discover Edi is medically unwell; their behaviour is unintentional. Your behaviour towards them changes – you have sympathy, show understanding and begin to develop a good rapport with them.

6. Interpersonal Relationships

The animal metaphors described in Chapter 4 are a useful adjunct to help identify problematic relationships. Chapter 9 goes on to explain the effect these instinctive reactions have on Edi but the following paragraphs serve as an introduction.

Strategies helpful in eating disorders differ from those that work for an acute illness without any emotional underpinnings. For instance, it is very unlikely to be effective if you try to argue against Edi's eating behaviour, to dominate and demand change (the 'Rhino response'). Indeed, this will probably make the situation worse. In order to help someone overcome their eating disorder, listening to and trying to understand their point of view is essential. Even if you can't understand how or why the individual is thinking and behaving the way they are, you can try to accept that this is how the sufferer feels at that moment.

The emotional tone may oscillate between and within family members – parents, siblings, grandparents, spouses, children – struggling to cope in the outside world of work and other activities while also trying to support Edi, often with little information or help. Unfortunately the extreme responses described – Kangaroo, Rhino, Jellyfish or Ostrich – though natural, can be harmful as they can result in rebellion or regression and even more entrenched eating disorder behaviours. Finding the correct balance of compassionate guidance within a warm relationship, whilst acknowledging the problems caused by the extremely challenging behaviour of the illness, is very difficult.

Remember the need for consistency which can be blown away by strong emotions. In the mantra of the carer, remember the three important Cs – *Calm, Consistent, Compassionate.*

- Beware of 'charging in for change', like a Rhinoceros

- Beware of trying to provide total protection, by trying to protect Edi in a Kangaroo's 'pouch'

- Beware of having your emotional responses on display like a Jellyfish

- Ignoring symptoms, hoping Edi will grow out of it, like an Ostrich with its head in the sand, will not help either

- Beware of striving too hard for peace and changing your life completely to accommodate the eating disorder symptoms

- Try, instead, to get alongside the sufferer and help guide in the right direction, rather like a Dolphin travelling alongside and helping to pilot a boat through stormy seas

- Think of yourself as a St Bernard rescue dog, calmly tracking out to providing warmth and nurture to Edi lost in the dangerous frozen wastes of an eating disorder.

7. Unmet Needs

(a) Caring for Your Own Needs

It is all too easy for each member of a family to feel overwhelmed by the power of the eating disorder. Families can become very isolated as they turn inwards in the struggle to cope.

Many carers do not feel entitled to take any time off for recharging their batteries. With symptoms possibly demanding attention many times a day over long periods, and affecting all aspects of home life, without remission and respite this is a heavy load. *Therefore, to avoid burnout and stress-related problems, it is important that carers take time to look after themselves and plan their own survival strategies so that they may continue to support the sufferer effectively.*

The most important thing carers can do is timetable some pleasurable activities into each week – meet up with friends, follow a hobby or interest either new or old – and make sure you do things for fun or which give a sense of personal achievement. You need to counterbalance the difficulties by having a store of positive experiences to draw upon. Draw up a list of your favourite things. Make time for some of them. This is a 'two for one' deal; not only does it stop your automatic defensive reflexes dominating (Jellyfish, Ostrich), but it models an emotionally intelligent way of being – Dolphin – which is a key message for the person with an eating disorder. Respite for you also has a further benefit for Edi: he or she is learning to cope for short times alone and thus slowly building confidence for the future.

Take care not to drift into cycles of unhelpful behaviours, e.g. drinking to block out how you feel, or isolating yourself by not seeing friends, or stopping doing outside activities – all of which are very easy to slide into when under pressure.

The pressures of caring may take a very heavy toll. Some carers may benefit from professional counselling themselves or may require a GP's advice with regard to a diagnosis of depression and the need for therapy themselves or prescription medication.

'Family therapy' – joint therapy with Edi and one or more family members – may help progress treatment and provide a forum for discussion. The result may be that all family members, particularly the main carer, feel the benefit of more support.

Try to timetable special time with Edi, such as a short walk, a joint game, a comedy video or perhaps a trip to the shops or cinema, etc., which will help you nurture the positive, rewarding and non-anorexic aspects of your relationship; unfortunately it is all too easy to lose sight of this. In other words, another C: **Cherish** yourself and your whole family.

Change will not happen overnight. It is important for you to set *gradual* goals in which you *slowly* establish a reduction in the amount – intensity and face-to-face hours – of care you give. Think of the Kangaroo . . .

Reviewing progress afterwards is an important part of re-establishing a measure of independence for the sufferer. No matter how small the step towards assuming personal responsibility, whether in nutritional matters or time without company, justified praise for what has been achieved can be given. If the goal has proved very difficult, praise can be given for the effort in trying. Progress reviews with professionals are also important, with the option of more intensive care if necessary.

(b) Caring for the Rest of the Family

It is difficult to find enough time for other family members, who can easily feel neglected. Also, your own stress may spill over into your interactions with them and you may sound more irritable and impatient.

Siblings may have developed their own – right or wrong – ideas about the illness and they may have patterns of interaction that are not helpful, e.g. retaliating to irrational anger. Often they blame themselves for not being able to help. They may become angry about their own neglected needs; they may be resentful about being obliged to accommodate to eating disorder behaviours; they may feel guilty about achieving normal milestones. (Some siblings deliberately under-achieve in order not to highlight any contrast between their development and that of the person with an eating disorder.) Others leave home as soon as they can.

It is important to try to address these issues if they arise. Children can understand that they may have to wait for time with parents but it is important not to overlook others in the family totally. Draw in other family members to help if you can. Siblings can play an important role by maintaining connections with life outside the eating disorder, such as making a trip to the cinema together, enjoying a walk, a trip to the local swimming pool, a drink out in a café or any other shared activity.

Sometimes the relationship remains difficult. Siblings may be very different sorts of people and may need to accept that they can never 'get it' with each other.

8. Stigma

Many psychiatric disorders are stigmatised by society, possibly in part because these difficulties are hard to understand and people are frightened by what they don't understand. As discussed earlier, the myth that eating problems are caused by the parents can shape your interactions with other people. Feelings of shame and blame can be particularly difficult to bear, and feelings of isolation may follow. However, avoiding friends and other people, on the assumption that they will also blame – and believe in the stigma associated with mental health problems – may give credence to the idea that it might indeed be the parents' fault.

Most friends are willing to help when a problem is shared. By never mentioning a problem, the opportunity of offering help and support is therefore denied to those who possibly could and would help. Sharing valuable 'time-out' activities such as chatting over a cup of tea, lunch out or cooking for a friend, all of which provide respite for carers, also provides ideal times to be heard and listened to.

Remember

There is no magic recipe that works in all cases. Rather, recovery is often a protracted, evolving process with you as a guide or coach.

Carers (both lay and professional) need to be open, to respect each other and aim to work in synchrony – much easier said than done because the eating disorder often produces strong differences of opinion among carers – Divide and Rule are the operating principles of this 'minx' who has taken over your loved one. A consistent approach is essential, otherwise it will do its best to take over your home and family.

Words by Venables, who had a clinic at Guy's Hospital where he cared for many cases of anorexia nervosa a hundred years ago, are still pertinent now:

> *No patient should remain uncured and no patient should be allowed to die. The doctor (carer) must never admit defeat and never lose his temper . . . the opportunities for annoyance will be many.*[1]

Patience and calmness – not common virtues in our striving western societies – are some of the key skills to help with this illness. In the face of the many 'opportunities for annoyance' noted by Venables a hundred years ago, they may be hard to develop.[1] Friends and family, finding a self-help group, finding spiritual help, can all provide important support. Understanding the science underpinning psychological principles can also help construct an environment in which the eating disorder does not flourish.

> *Working together slowly but surely, calmly and consistently, brings results – though not overnight.*

ACTION POINTS ➤

- Ensure you have time to **cherish** the whole family. Think about how you can plan pleasurable activities. Maximise the joy of everyday things, appreciate and relish the beauty of your surroundings, e.g. you might want to pick or buy flowers for the meal table, take time to watch a spectacular sunset, take a short walk in the sunshine.

- Maintain as many links with people outside the family as possible. **Cherish** your social network. **Communicate** with others.

- Spend time with Edi to 'rekindle' and encourage their 'well side'.

⬅ REFLECTION POINTS

1. Actively planning strategies to ensure that you can master the elements needed in your role as a caregiver is extremely important to enable and ensure effective caring.

2. This can be a 'Two for One' deal – not only will you lessen the strain of the care-giving role, the indirect effect is the opportunity to model for Edi how to master difficulties by self-care.

3. Remember the key Cs to the whole process – Calmness, Compassion, Consistency, Cherishing, Communication and making and maintaining Connections.

Reference List

1. Venables, J.F. *Guy's Hospital Report 80*, 213–22214. 1–1–1930.

6

Consequences – understanding medical risk

Important Observations

Most people living with someone with an eating disorder are terrified about the medical dangers, and the long- and short-term consequences of poor nutrition. It is helpful, in discussion with medical professionals, if you can be specific about what observations worry you. It can also be useful to jot any examples down, with any relevant details such as how often you've observed this, when it happened, etc. (At a later stage, you will, it is hoped, also be able to look back and appreciate progress.)

Finding a balance between being mindful of the medical risk that your loved one faces, and not panicking over what may or may not be important from a medical point of view, is often very difficult. This chapter offers basic guidance which may be discussed with an experienced professional on what to look out for, what it means, and when to call for help.

Body Mass Index

A term used by health professionals as a measure of weight in all patients, not just those with eating disorders, is Body Mass Index **(BMI)**. This is a form of volume measurement, calculated by dividing weight in kilograms by the square of height in metres.

BMI is a rough estimate of medical risk. By finding out Edi's weight (in kg) and height (in m), the chart on the following website can be used to predict their degree of medical risk: www.bmj.com/cgi/content/full/317/7170/1401.

Factors such as age (child, adolescent or adult), height and sex modify the risk and so this is an approximate measure only. BMI increases during development in young adolescents (puberty) and it is useful to use standard charts that show the expected BMI range for each age (e.g. the aforementioned chart).

In addition to the absolute measure of BMI, other factors that can contribute to risk include:

- the rate at which weight is falling;

- whether behaviours such as the use of laxatives and vomiting are present;

- if there are pre-existing medical conditions, e.g. diabetes.

Regular Weight Monitoring

An important part of the treatment of anorexia nervosa is to monitor medical risk regularly, by measuring weight. Both professionals and family members should be aware that during the illness, some sufferers may try to persuade other people that their weight is greater than it actually is by using devious ploys, such as secreting weights/batteries on their person or drinking large amounts of liquid, etc. (Pro-anorexia websites give details of most of these tricks, and sometimes eating disordered individuals will exchange information on these.) Thus weight or BMI alone is not a satisfactory measure of risk and a more complex analysis of how the body is functioning is needed. On the IOP website there is a document which looks at a variety of bodily functions in order to produce a more detailed measure of medical risk (see www.iop.kcl.ac.uk/IoP/Departments/PsychMed/EDU/downloads/pdf/RiskAssessment.pdf).

Regular weight checks can be carried out by the GP or by the practice nurse. This can be supplemented by checks on body temperature, circulation, muscle strength (these may involve, for instance, a 'squat test' where someone is asked to squat then get up without using their arms as levers), pulse, blood pressure, and blood tests for any deficiency in essential nutrients.

All the checks above are discussed with a sufferer, along with what they mean in relation to their physical health. If the results of these checks place an individual at high risk, then there is a need to reflect about what steps are required to improve their health. A sufferer is the only person who can really take those steps.

Your GP/practice nurse will keep a regular record of Edi's weight fluctuations. You may, for your own security and peace of mind, need to keep a weight chart/diary for yourself. This may have a positive or a negative response from Edi depending on the individual and their attitude towards and beliefs about their illness at that point in time. Some sufferers will keep their weekly weights a secret – angry and unwilling to let on whether their illness has won, or not, in terms of the scale's reading. Others may adopt an open attitude, appreciating their progress by the charting and displaying of results. Some families and sufferers find home scales beneficial for weight monitoring. For others, Edi's obsession with weight means that scales around the house are unhelpful, distressing and a hindrance to progress. You must work out a weight monitoring system that suits you AND Edi.

ACTION POINTS ➔

CONTACT your GP (a note/letter might be easier than the phone, and can be kept for reference with other patient notes) to report any of the following. The sufferer should be medically examined if you notice these symptoms:

- Your loved one is always so cold that she or he needs the heating on constantly, and/or wears several layers of clothes even when others find it too hot.

skills-based learning for caring for a loved one

- You notice that hands and feet look blue and cold – this is a sign of circulation problems.

- Your loved one is dizzy and faint after standing up quickly or you notice puffiness around the eyes in the morning, and/or swollen ankles in the afternoon. All of the above can signify salt and water imbalance.

- Your loved one has difficulty climbing stairs, or brushing their hair, or raising their arms for any length of time. This is due to muscle strength being affected by the illness.

PHONE your GP or get emergency help if your loved one:

- Becomes breathless on lying flat

- Develops a very fast heart rate

- Has a seizure

- Becomes sleepy or twitchy*

- Complains of pins and needles in their toes*

- Hands twist into a spasm.*

Note: * These indicate serious salt imbalance.

Be cautious at times of particular danger:

- If the routine changes and meals are delayed or missed (e.g. long journeys)

- After excessive exercising

- When starting to feed again (this needs to be taken slowly with small portions of normal food taken at regular intervals throughout the day with vitamin and mineral supplements).

These are general guidelines. *Your gut feelings are also important – note anything which concerns you for later discussion.*

Important Changes – Talking It Over with Edi

Skills of positive communication and assertiveness (Chapter 8) are needed when discussing risk with your loved one. This involves:

- Voicing your concerns
- Stating clearly what action you have taken
- Offering to help.

The conversation may go something like this:

> *'I have noticed several things which have made me worry about your health. First, you are very sensitive to cold – you have the fire turned on in your room so that it feels like a furnace. Also, I've noticed that you find opening heavy doors difficult. I'd like you to go and have a medical check-up to put my mind at rest. Could I help by making you an appointment with our GP? If you want me to, I'd be happy to come with you.'*

The essence is to stay calm but to list your concerns with compassion.

Mental Health Act

The Mental Health Act exists to protect people who cannot understand the danger to their health; when this happens a person may be admitted to hospital against their will. Gentle persuasion of the need for specialist hospital care, perhaps trying some of the suggestions in this book such as the 'Readiness Ruler' (see Chapter 7, 'Understanding Change'), may work, whereas confrontation may drive Edi further into entrenched resistance. In very extreme circumstances, after attempts at gentle persuasion, if there is evidence of high medical risk to Edi and their condition has become life-threatening, it may be necessary to use this Act and admit the person to hospital against their will. Further information about the MHA and its use may be obtained from the IOP website (www.eatingresearch.com).

Starvation as a Maintaining Factor

Above we outlined how anorexia can put life acutely in jeopardy because of inadequate nutrition, and in Chapter 3 we describe how starvation can interfere with brain maturation, making it more difficult to recover from the illness.

Adolescence is a time of important changes in brain function. Developmental changes include the ability to have an overview of mental capacities, to think abstractly and reflectively and to monitor some of the more automatic aspects of brain function. Similar skills develop in emotional intelligence. Poor nutrition during this phase can inhibit this process and so the brain remains in the immature state. Prolonged poor nutrition at this phase can freeze brain development, which makes recovery difficult. This highlights the importance of restoring adequate nutrition in a sustained manner as early as is possible in the course of the illness.

ACTION POINTS ➡

- If you are concerned about Edi's symptoms, jot down examples. When did it happen? For how long? How often? etc.

- Report to your GP, by letter, or phone if urgent, giving relevant details.

- Establish a routine for regular weight monitoring.

- Talk with Edi:
  - voice your concerns
  - explain your actions
  - offer help.

REFLECTION POINTS

1. Be mindful of risk and recruit help to manage this if necessary.

2. Prolonged poor nutrition interferes with maturation, impeding recovery.

3. The regulation of emotion, abstract and social intelligence is affected by prolonged poor nutrition, again creating barriers to recovery.

skills-based learning for caring for a loved one

7

Understanding change

Introduction

Changing *any* behaviour is usually not a simple switch between two options; '*Today I usually do this – but tomorrow I'm going to change completely and do this instead*'. There are usually many steps in between, depending upon our circumstances, the environment, other people's demands, what we see as the pros and cons of changing and whether we feel confident that we can accomplish change. There are several psychological models that describe how people change their behaviour. In this section we discuss what is known in theory about change, especially relating to major life-affecting decisions. Addictive and compulsive behaviours can be particularly difficult to change, as adaptations and anomalies in automatic brain processes can obscure the underlying issues.

Stages of Change

Changing eating disorder behaviours is a complex process. It usually involves passing through a stage where the person stubbornly resists any idea about change. This stubborn resistance to even considering changing behaviour, seeing no need for change despite the concern expressed by family and friends, can be called '*Precontemplation*'. The next stage involves moving on to a time when the person is 'in two minds' about the need to change, a stage of motivation when 'Contemplation' of change replaces absolute denial of even the need for, or possibility of, change. In 'Contemplation', juggling thoughts about the pros and cons of change begins, and whether there is enough confidence that change can be followed through. Then comes consideration of change, with all the difficulties being recognised, and development of personal determination to at least try to change behaviour-causing problems. Contemplation, followed by recognition and acknowledgement of the challenges ahead, it is hoped will lead into 'Action' – and the beginning of real change. 'Maintenance' of change is another particular challenge as the triggers and positive aspects of the old behaviour remain, and there may be many setbacks. The various stages of change are illustrated below and opposite.

TABLE 7.1 Stages of Change in Eating Disorders

Stage 1: *Precontemplation*. In this situation Edi has only one mindset – their eating disorder seems to be a solution, offering rewards without any perceived costs.

Stage 2: *Contemplation*. In this stage Edi is in two minds, seeing the costs and problems that the eating disorder brings but also aware of the rewards and positive aspects, seeing all the obstacles that changing will bring, and oscillating between these two mindsets of change or no change. It is a time of confusion and distress.

Stage 3: *Determination and difficulties*. In this stage the resolution of the conflict favours moving away from the eating disorder. The costs, of remaining with the eating disorder, are seen to outweigh the benefits.

Stage 4: *Action*. In this stage Edi will have made some steps towards getting help or making changes. However, there is often a physical and psychological rebound of all the things that have been suppressed and so progress is stormy.

Stage 5: *Maintenance*. In this stage Edi consolidates and builds on previous progress. However, developing new connections with the world without the eating disorder takes time and effort.

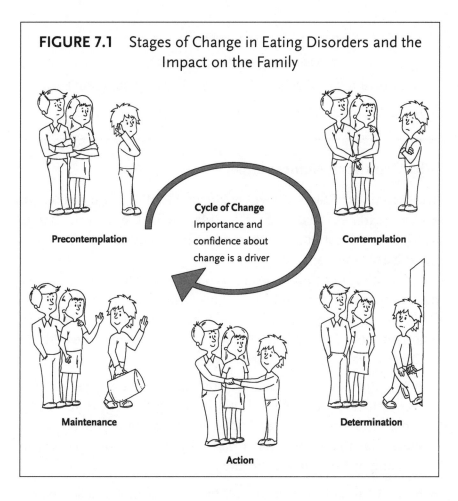

FIGURE 7.1 Stages of Change in Eating Disorders and the Impact on the Family

Precontemplation

Contemplation

Cycle of Change
Importance and confidence about change is a driver

Maintenance

Determination

Action

Edi may go through each stage several times before lasting progress is maintained – don't be too discouraged when setbacks occur; this is part of the illness pattern. New things are learnt with each setback and restart. Keep going on the strategies and techniques outlined in this book; actively look for the support needed to continue your caring role effectively.

Although it can be helpful to think in terms of stages, it also can be helpful to think of change in terms of a dimension. The '*Readiness Ruler*' illustrates this concept:

Measuring readiness to change

Not interested in change   *Eager to put change into place*

0------1------2------3------4------5------6------7------8------9------10

Why Use the 'Readiness Ruler'?

The 'Readiness Ruler' (above) is a useful tool that you can use to explore readiness to change. The Ruler opens the door to change as you ask questions which focus the discussion on problem solving and solutions.

Is Edi ready to change? Would you place your loved one's readiness to change at the right-hand side of the Readiness Ruler (ready for Action?) Or perhaps Edi is in Precontemplation, and totally adamant there is no need to change? Or somewhere in the middle?

Other advantages to using the Ruler include:

- A tangible way of reviewing progress – 'that shows you are really moving on. Fantastic! Two weeks ago, you gave yourself a score of 2 on the Ruler, today you're putting yourself at 4. Please let me know what I can help you to do to keep you thinking at 4 or move on further.'

- A practical tool with which you both can play, and talk around, avoiding a confrontational approach that can often emerge from eye-to-eye contact.

- The Ruler can be adapted for any behaviour or symptom of eating disorder (see Chapter 11, 'Managing Undereating', Chapter 12, 'How to Help with Overeating' and Chapter 13, 'Managing Difficult Behaviours').

- Although it may seem rather formal it can help structure a conversation and will stop you falling into any of the Kangaroo, Jellyfish, Rhino or Ostrich traps, becoming over-emotional, trying to argue logically against the illogical thinking of the illness, and so on.

- If carers recognise, in their own behaviour, elements of Kangaroo or any of the other personalities described, the Readiness Ruler may be a handy way of thinking towards replacing that behaviour and what might better help achieve the change.

ACTION POINT ➤

Make a guess yourself about what rating you would give Edi on this line. Then ask your partner/friend also to make a guess. Following this, discuss with each other the reasons that you have given this score. Come up with specific examples of what you have observed to illustrate exactly why you would give this score. Try not to be swayed too much by subjective judgements or what Edi has said; think more about what has been done, and your observations. If you cannot agree at this point, or remain uncertain, plan to review after a period and discuss again.

It is also helpful to find some time to do this exercise jointly with Edi.

Saying It

People tend to act in a way that is consistent with what *they have said out loud to an audience*.

The Readiness Ruler is a useful listening device in opening the way for an exploration of ideas as it can promote 'change talk'; it demonstrates a recognised psychological rule in understanding how people change – that if someone has talked about even the possibility of making a change, it is more likely that they will follow through with action.

A constant complaint of people with eating disorders is that no one listens to them. Indeed, we often all 'tune out' to 'eating disorder talk' as the compulsive aspects – for instance, prolonged descriptions of recipes and their respective merits lasting hours –

are so obviously unhelpful. Also, reinforcing this type of talk by giving it our time and attention is unhelpful.

However, at the same time, listening and talking about non-eating disorder things, or possibilities of change from the eating disorder behaviour, is essential. Therefore listening carefully for these more healthy topics interwoven into the unhealthy focus on eating and food, and eliciting and development of even the *possibility* of change to more healthy behaviours, is an important skill for carers to develop.

Aspects of Change

There are two aspects of readiness to change. The first is *how IMPORTANT change is to the individual*, and the second is *how CONFIDENT the individual is that change can be tackled.*

Carers challenging some of their own behaviours in relationship to the eating disorder need to stand back, trust and allow Edi to take responsibility and develop their own skills too. This is essential but difficult as it will involve watching powerlessly whilst Edi makes mistakes, suffers setbacks and encounters difficulties. Carers may feel less than confident about preventing themselves rushing in to provide Kangaroo protection on seeing commitment to change faltering, or be tempted again to try the logical argument route of Rhino. If not successful in the first few attempts, *don't give up, keep calm* and *allow time* for Edi to develop and consolidate his or her skills.

EXAMPLE:

Edi – 'I have given myself 5 because I know that one of my ambitions is to have a family and I know that it is out of the question at this weight.'

Carer – 'You're anxious about your future. You are worried that having an eating disorder may have future implications for having a family.'

TABLE 7.2 Small Steps to Change with the Readiness Ruler

- Start by asking Edi to give him or herself a score on the Readiness Ruler.

- Talk about both their global readiness to change – how important is it to them? And, their confidence in their abilities to instigate change.

- Then open up the conversation by saying '*I am interested that you have given yourself that score. What makes you give yourself that score rather than, say, 0?*'

- Listen carefully to what is said. Ask what score on the Ruler she or he thinks you might give. Ask her or him why she or he thinks this. Again listen carefully to the replies.

- Then say what score you would actually give, and state your reasons – your specific observations – why you think this. This will help initiate talk about change.

- Remember – try to steer a conversation so that *Edi* – rather than you – gives the arguments for change. Listen out for *any* change talk and then try to summarise what has been said. A repetition and reflection of change statements serves to emphasise them.

- Remember – change is more likely when an individual has voiced the desire or need for change.

Edi's replies reflect clearly the concern the individual experiences (or not). Reflecting on what Edi tells you is a clear behavioural marker that you have *listened.*

The conversation may then flow on to what would need to happen or what help would be required to get to a higher score.

> '*What do you think might have to happen for you to get a higher score?*'

By the end of this exercise you may have heard some elements of commitment to change to build on. If not, after a period of time calmly try again. Perhaps mention that '*The doctor/therapist feels that your nutritional health is at risk . . . let's try the Readiness Ruler again. What score do you think you might give yourself now?'* Again follow the Small Steps through.

Next Steps

> '*Is there any help I can give that would enable you to move nearer to the 10 side of the spectrum?'*

This offer of social support promotes change and can get people thinking about help and support towards change – they are not alone in the struggle. Even if a gentle offer of support is initially refused, Edi may think about it and return later to the idea – try to keep all lines of communication open to the possibility of change.

This exercise can be repeated on several occasions and used for many different types of unwelcome behaviours in eating disorders including obsessive compulsive rituals, vomiting or use of laxatives.

In summary, the aim of the Readiness Ruler exercise is to help your loved one reflect on their eating disorder and how it may affect their life both currently and in the future. This will involve trying to understand the mixed feelings that Edi has about the illness and about change. Many of the positive (perceived by Edi) and negative aspects of an eating disorder are unconscious or inaccessible. It is important to keep listening in order to understand the forces that keep the eating disorder fixed. Listen to find where and when there are openings and opportunities for providing further information and help. Grab those moments!

Although remember – it is common for people to go up and down the Readiness Ruler, backwards and forwards through these various stages of change several times.

Carers Who Want to Change

Carers who recognise in themselves behaviour which might be unhelpful – Kangaroo, Rhino, Ostrich, Jellyfish – in supporting Edi's struggle with the compulsions may also find it helpful to rate their own attitudes to difficult behaviours that affect their lives as well as Edi's. There are several questions to reflect on with your partner or a friend – how **interested** are you for Edi to change? How **important** to you is it that she or he changes as soon as possible? How **confident** do you feel that you can help Edi change? You may want to make guesses about each other's scores and then check with each other how correct you are.

How interested are you for Edi to change?
Not interested in change   Eager to put change into place
0------1------2------3------4------5------6------7------8------9------10

How important for you is it for Edi to change?
Not important   Very important
0------1------2------3------4------5------6------7------8------9------10

How confident do you feel you can help Edi to change?
No confidence   Very confident
0------1------2------3------4------5------6------7------8------9------10

Differing Scores and Differing Opinions

What happens when you are keen and confident that Edi can change, and soon, but Edi has other ideas? If they are not yet ready for change, give themselves a score of 1 and are firmly stuck in the 'precontemplative' phase? A metaphor involving dodgem cars can act as a useful adjunct to demonstrate possible conflicting opinions.

For example, you may not be willing or able to think about discussing change with Edi. You may find it unbearable to see how

FIGURE 7.2   Guess Which Might Illustrate Rhino or Ostrich?

Score 1–4
Avoidance
Edi goes off rails

Score 5–8
Calm, compassion
Safe, nudging as Dolphin
Warm, nurturing as St Bernard

Score 9–10
Conflict
Edi battles on

upset she or he gets when you apply *any* sort of pressure, no matter how gentle, and eventually resort to avoiding the issue (Ostrich). Or, it may be that you have your own hang-ups about eating – you may even have had an eating disorder yourself. Consequently, you find yourself colluding with Edi's illness – you are over-accommodating to their behaviour and over-sympathetic (Kangaroo). Alternatively, the whole situation becomes too emotional for you and Edi ends up being a witness to this (Jellyfish). All these feelings will lead you to have mixed views about discussing change with Edi. *Be careful that they do not lead to Edi relentlessly getting deeper into the eating disorder with prolonged symptoms.*

In contrast, you may be determined that Edi will change as soon as possible . . . it seems a simple solution – just eat! – and you will give yourself a score of 10. *The problem with a carer having such a high score level of drive and determination is that it can lead into head-to-head conflict with Edi, which may lead to him or her getting even more stuck* (Rhinoceros reaction).

The ideal position is if you can be determined and persistent in your attempts to help Edi change by being willing to take the time to listen, to try to see their perspective and to go at their pace – rather than trying to push and shove – by gently guiding and motivating towards change (Dolphin). Work TOGETHER. The aphorism from **beat** about change in eating disorders, '*You alone can do it, but you can't do it alone*', is very true.

It can be a source of distress if everyone has highly divergent scores, especially if these are not talked about but just acted on. The main advantage of using a Readiness Ruler is that the scores are seen overtly. Following discussion about any differences, an agreement can be made to disagree whilst respecting everyone's current perspective, i.e. 'I can see that you are not ready to change yet'. (Please note the use of *yet*. It is important to hold an optimistic 'can do' frame of mind, and so temper extreme statements by using modifiers 'yet', 'at the moment', 'with the present perspective', 'currently', which leaves the door open for a possible change of heart and mind at a later date.)

> '*I understand that it is entirely up to you whether you decide to change or not. However the illness does affect the family, your relationships with friends and at work, as well as your future, and so I am drawn in.*'

How People Move Towards Change

The theory underlying the mechanisms by which people can move along the dimensions of change is based on common sense but there is also psychological research evidence backing it up.

There are two main principles. People become more ready to change if:

1. *It is important for them to change*, i.e. the positive benefits for change outweigh the negative aspects of change.

2. *They are confident that they can change.*

Described in this section is the way we can move people towards change within individual treatment, giving ideas on which carers can base home interactions with Edi.

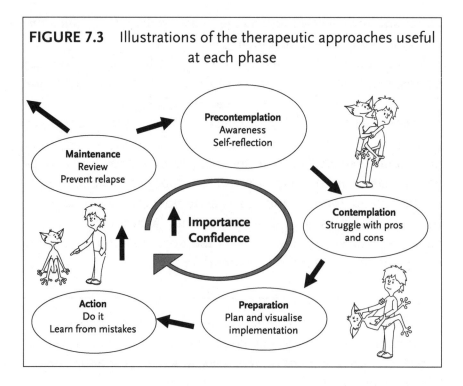

FIGURE 7.3 Illustrations of the therapeutic approaches useful at each phase

Precontemplation
Awareness
Self-reflection

Maintenance
Review
Prevent relapse

Importance
Confidence

Contemplation
Struggle with pros
and cons

Action
Do it
Learn from mistakes

Preparation
Plan and visualise
implementation

For someone in *Precontemplation* the work involved is towards thinking about the importance of change. This is tackled from as wide a perspective as possible. Edi is asked to think about how anorexia or other eating disorders fits with their overall beliefs and values about life both in the past and present, raising awareness and self-reflection. Carers, whether home or professional, will be trying to help Edi step back from the detailed focus on eating and symptoms to consider the bigger picture of his or her life story, and will need to remain calm and patient in this phase. Edi may feel very confused after seeming to make some progress, but then fix rigidly on some eating disorder detail. *The more carers can remain calm and consistent (like the St Bernard) in keeping connections going and open channels of communication in this phase, the more successful progress is likely to be towards reaching contemplation of change.* If frustration at lack of progress threatens to overwhelm, carers may like to take 'time out' – a walk perhaps –

rather than risk reinforcing Precontemplation, and try again at a later date when a suitable opportunity can be found.

In *Contemplation* we try to make some of the negative aspects of an eating disorder more salient and obvious, exploring ways in which the positive benefits of an eating disorder can be attained from other means that do not impact so negatively on the quality of life of the individual and his or her family, and working to bolster self-esteem so that the individual is confident that they can make the changes. This is done by showing respect for their ideas and beliefs, and then working to shape their ideas towards change, by paying attention to those beliefs which will help the change process and ignoring those that may interrupt it. At the same time we respect their autonomy, by stressing their right to choose for themselves. In this phase the confusion can be cleared a little by connecting with the thoughts, emotions and values that are on the side of change while also being respectful, non-judgemental and **compassionate** with those thoughts, emotions and values on the side of no change.

Once there is a **commitment** to change, it is possible to set up small behavioural experiments which lead to the attainment of new goals. When people are in *Preparation* we try to help them develop a detailed visualisation of change goals with great attention to detail about implementation – actual planning of how the changes might be managed. One of the goals is to be more flexible and to learn to adjust to a sudden change, for instance in developing a goal.

Once in *Action*, an interactive learning cycle develops. This involves review and reflection on what has been achieved, and consolidation of new learning and perspectives into a new construction of self in the world.

Families and other carers have an important part to play in helping with this process of change in different settings.

Maintaining Factors for an Eating Disorder

Eating disorders, in particular anorexia nervosa, tend to persist and are difficult to treat. For Edi, their eating disorder comes to serve some sort of function or be of vital importance. Through discussion, people with an eating disorder eventually are able to understand and reflect on the possibility that they gain some perceived benefits from the illness. For example, at the Maudsley, when we asked our patients to write letters to 'Anorexia, their friend', they wrote that the illness makes them feel safe; it can make them feel special; it can stifle and suppress emotions and yet serve to signal to other people, in an indirect way, that something is wrong.

People with eating disorders, particularly anorexia, seem to have a characteristic cognitive style or share certain personality features. For example, sufferers tend to be over-analytical, seeing only the detail, rather than being able to synthesise the moment into the tapestry of life. They lose sight of the overarching aim of life as they become trapped with their compulsive behaviours and rituals. Additionally, people with eating disorders have a tendency to be rather single-minded, enabling them to focus on one thing without distraction. The down side of this is increasing inflexibility and rigidity. Such a strategy serves another benefit: to help them avoid thinking or dealing with painful issues about themselves, stressful events, or their connections within the world and other people; a very powerful illness-maintaining factor indeed.

← REFLECTION POINTS

1. Unlike most people who are ill, people with an eating disorder often do not recognise that they have a problem and do not want to change.

2. Conflict and frustration are lessened if expectations are paced with the readiness to change.

3. The odds of change occurring are increased if *Edi* is given the opportunity and encouraged to talk about change in him or herself.

4. It is important to have a stance that remains optimistic and yet is not too pushy for change.

5. The more carers, both home and professional, can be warm, calm and compassionate the more confidence Edi will gain that she or he can initiate and maintain change.

8

Communication

This chapter is lengthy and deals with the important concept of Communication. The beginning of the chapter (pp. 64–70) gives an overview of the communication process and some concise ideas for those who lack confidence in this area. The latter part of the chapter takes the carer through different 'communication skills' topics. These skills will further develop your resources to steer Edi, in the long term, towards recovery and health and, in the short term, improve home life, atmosphere and family relationships. Each skill will take time, practice and patience to learn. Do not try to take in everything at once!

How Communication Happens

In everyday life most conversations are practical exchanges, such as: 'Will you be back for tea tonight?' or 'Where's my blue shirt?' Most words are chosen on a functional and perhaps careless basis; most conversations are not particularly planned or designed to build or develop relationships constructively – although tone, context and accompanying body language in any conversation, or even sentence, may indeed add to or detract from the existing relationship. Added to the actual words spoken, plus tone, context, body language and so on, will be how the words are received; this will again depend not only on tone, etc. but also on how the hearer is feeling at that moment. There may be times when even the most innocuous remark may strike a chord, resulting in an unexpected reaction.

The following diagram can illustrate the various points where things might go wrong. When emotions run high and thinking becomes tunnel-visioned, as in living with eating disorders, it is easy for this process to slip. In such situations it is even more important to take care; to allocate time to reflect and to repair as soon as possible any inadvertent ruptures.

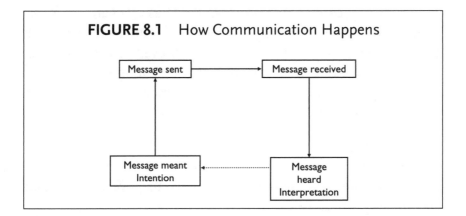

FIGURE 8.1   How Communication Happens

Some Starter Points for 'Communication Beginners'

Building Self-confidence

When family life includes a member suffering from an eating disorder, communication often becomes fraught. Conversations become derailed because the confidence of someone with an eating disorder has reached rock bottom, leading to distorted understanding of what is meant: where interest is intended, criticism may be assumed; where loving concern is intended, intrusion may be assumed. Coaching conversations which use a great deal of reflective listening can help prevent being at cross purposes in this way.

With a sufferer's self-confidence very low, carers can act as coaches helping to rebuild self-esteem, fostering the belief that Edi too can be effective in his or her own life. This can be done by helping the sufferer notice aspects of themselves – their abilities and skills, tasks they have successfully completed both currently and in the past. Gradually, by taking every opportunity to increase warmth in the relationships, by 'modelling' or showing by their own example, carers can support their loved one towards gradually learning to think better of themselves. By doing so they can help their loved ones develop the effective self-nurturance and emotional intelligence needed to beat the illness.

As in every other part of life, it will not be possible to make every conversation 'deep and meaningful'; in eating disorders it is important for carers to seek opportunities actively to foster motivation towards changing difficult behaviours affecting health and well-being. This will not be a one-off event but an ongoing process of encouragement on what may be a long road. A target of five minutes a day at least – preferably more – may be a good goal to aim for.

Think of VIEW

Notice and comment on the good things that Edi does and give praise for them – wherever possible use Very Important Encouraging Words (VIEW).

It is helpful to develop 'Useful Sentences' to draw attention to progress. This may at first feel a bit awkward, therefore it is worth practising – perhaps with a friend, or in a mirror – so that they come more and more easily when you need them.

'Thank you for . . .'
'I noticed that you . . .'
'I really like it when you . . .' [name it – help me tidy up, keep your room tidy, bring in the washing, put out the bin – *anything* you can praise, no matter how small.]
'I can see you're trying hard.'
'I know how difficult this is for you [name it – e.g. finishing a meal or snack, refraining from visiting the bathroom immediately after a meal, cleaning up after a binge] *and really appreciate how hard you are trying.'*

Additionally, make special efforts to offer physical displays of love and affection; reach out to show you recognise and value the person, whilst still acknowledging the effects of the eating disorder.

The Family's Role

Within families we all break the rules about good communication – we may interrupt each other, we may assume we know what another family member's reaction will be without actually discussing the matter. We have such busy lives that we often do not take the time or trouble to really listen to each other. We assume that we can mind-read or that we know best. . . . Once you have the problem of an eating disorder in the family it is particularly important and necessary to follow all the rules of good communication. A constant refrain of individuals with an eating disorder is that people do not listen – however, you need to use the right sort of listening, and listen to the right things.

To cope with all the difficulties an eating disorder can bring, families need to function as a well-run committee! It is helpful to set aside time regularly so all can talk to each other in a *calm* controlled atmosphere (*NB not during meals*). This can be done formally with a set time and place free from interruptions, or it may be more informal, e.g. making sure that carers are around at a particular time and are relaxed with time to spare, perhaps reading papers on Sunday morning, a short walk to the bus stop, etc. Can you think of a good time and place for your own family and circumstances?

BOX 8.1 Some Ground Rules for Good Communication

1. Only one person speaks at a time.

2. Give Edi the opportunity to talk about change and the bigger picture, with encouragement to talk about life without an eating disorder as much as possible, e.g.

I'm interested in what you remember of our trip to see . . .
I'd like to hear more about . . .

3. If possible, allow Edi to have the majority of the speaking time, especially when the talk is of *change*, away from the eating disorder. *In usual practice all family members should have an equal time to speak but, as discussed in Chapter 7, change is more likely to occur if Edi has the opportunity to talk about it.*

4. The rule is not to get on a soapbox and deliver a standard script but to work at really understanding what each person is saying.

5. The atmosphere should be *calm, compassionate*, warm and respectful.

6. Try to keep the focus on the positive side, i.e. glass half full rather than half empty, by referring to any achievements and progress, no matter how small.

Listening

Listening to each other and understanding what the other is saying sounds easy. In fact, it is very difficult and takes skill and practice. If we are listening we need to *give non-verbal signs* – eye-contact, a nod perhaps or shake of the head, 'attention sounds' such as *mmmmm* and *uh-huh* – that we are attending to the speaker. A good way of proving that we are listening is to test whether a *summary or a précis of what we have heard* fits what the speaker means. This may even just be a simple repetition of what the speaker has said but it is best if you put it into your own words – rather than risk sounding like a tape-recorder. A summary of what you think has been said and meant can be a useful way of clarifying the content. Often meaning and understanding of words and concepts can be used idiosyncratically, with meaning dependent on the listener's background, experience, vocabulary and use of that vocabulary, state of alertness or tiredness. In summarising, it does not matter if you do not get it quite right. In some ways it is helpful to get it a bit wrong and mistake the individual's meaning, as that can lead the speaker to add more detail and repeat their thoughts.

The important thing about listening is to show that you are willing to give the time and energy to try to understand. Not only does this signify listening but it gives the speaker a chance to reflect on what they have said. Often we do not know what we think until we say it! Listening carefully, with reflection of what you hear, allows Edi to recognise, and put into words, thoughts. As behaviour change is more likely to follow expression in words of thoughts of change, you want Edi to *talk about change as much as possible*.

Getting It Wrong: Mistakes and Treasures

Here we diverge to discuss another important truism from audit research which is also true about caring for someone with an eating disorder – *'Every mistake is a treasure'*. One of the core vulnerabilities of people with eating disorders is that they are overly concerned about making mistakes and so they become trapped within a predictable, error-free, cage. If, as a carer, you can show that you are not frightened of admitting that you have made a mistake, that you are willing to think about what you have learned from it, and that you can be flexible enough to shift your approach in the light of new learning, then you are transmitting an important life skill.

Involving Emotions

Change can be promoted if the emotional tone is *warm and accepting*. You may be angry towards the eating disorder part of your loved one but remember that Edi is much more than merely the eating disorder; Edi still has a non-eating disorder part too, no matter how deeply buried for the moment. Try hard to focus on the bigger-picture aspects of your loved one as an individual separate from the illness part; give your loved one as much love, care, encouragement and warmth as you can.

Communication Skill 1: Motivational Interviewing

The following list of Do's and Don'ts is based on an examination of the interactions from hundreds of therapeutic sessions which form the skills used in a psychological approach called 'motivational interviewing', an important part of treatment of eating disorders at the Maudsley Hospital. This approach was developed in order to work effectively with people who do not want to change, for instance in addictions or alcoholism. You may find reading the textbooks that describe this approach helpful.[1,2,3]

Don't

- Argue, lecture or persuade with logic
- Assume an authoritarian or expert role
- Order, direct, warn or threaten
- Do most of the talking
- Make moral statements, criticise, preach or judge
- Ask a series of (three) questions in a row
- Tell Edi that they have a problem
- Prescribe solutions or a certain course of action.

Do

- Let Edi present the arguments for change, give the opportunity to talk about, and hopefully resolve, ambivalence
- Focus on your loved one's concerns

- Emphasise that Edi has the choice and responsibility for deciding future behaviour

- Explore and reflect upon Edi's perception of the situation

- Reflect what you think you have heard with statements starting with you: *'You feel . . .'*, *'you think . . .'*

- Summarise periodically

- Aim to be as warm and loving as possible

- Beware of hostility and criticism.

The listening, motivational approach may seem very different from the role that carers have been used to, leading to feelings of frustration as you have to bite your tongue and not immediately offer your expertise and wisdom, or curb instincts to take over care. (Remember the animal metaphors!) Carers need to allow Edi to have a platform from which to experiment with and express what she or he thinks. The best way for Edi to do this is if there is an outside audience allowing a reflective test bed of ideas.

'LESS is more' is the spirit of motivational interviewing.

LESS is the key to this approach:

- L – *Listen*

- E – *Empathy not sympathy*

- S – *Share* non-eating disorder parts of life

- S – *Support*; increase confidence.

L – Listen   Listening conveys respect for another person's views and emotions. With Edi focused on food and shape, try to tap into the deeper meanings behind that talk – food and shape talk is usually a metaphor for emotional distress or negative beliefs about the self. People with an eating disorder often have quite strong beliefs that they themselves are deeply flawed or unworthy.

Some of the beliefs, thinking, and talking about food and shape, cover up:

- *'I hate myself; no one could possibly love me.'*
- *'I'm not worthy of love.'*
- *'Showing feelings is wrong.'*
- *'People will think I'm stupid if I say anything.'*
- *'I'm not good enough.'*
- *'I feel different to other people.'*
- *'I don't belong here.'*
- *'I'm different/weird/a freak.'*
- *'Life is threatening.'*
- *'It's wrong to ask for what I want: I must please others.'*
- *'Everyone is better than I am.'*
- *'Other people are luckier than I am.'*
- *'I must be strong and brave.'*
- *'Being frightened or crying is weak.'*
- *'I must be perfect.'*
- *'I must feel guilty for what I've done.'*
- *'I must not make mistakes or ask for help, that would be failing.'*
- *'It's wrong to have pleasure.'*
- *'I don't trust others.'*

skills-based learning for caring for a loved one

Do not get drawn into a dialogue about food, weight or shape, but rather say something like: 'It sounds as if you are upset'. Remember – carers need to demonstrate the skill of being able to step back from detail. Whenever tempted to join in a discussion about food or shape or weight *STOP, step back, withdraw*: 'I can hear you talking to me about eating disorder concerns. It sounds as if you are terrified.'

In order to show you are really listening, try to avoid letting loose a battery of questions, which only indicates you are demanding to shape the interaction and to be in control. If you are really listening you will have one or two questions but then encourage the person to talk more, to clarify what they are saying by making a précis or summary of what they have said.

E – Empathy   Empathy means trying to step into the other person's shoes and to see things from their perspective and to understand their emotional response. Give empathy not sympathy – sympathy implies that Edi is a passive helpless victim – *this illness can only be cured when Edi takes an active role and develops and practises the courage and stamina to withstand the compulsive concerns.*

Following the **C** agenda it is important to speak with *compassion*, a similar concept to empathy. Only Edi can decide when and how to change. Some parents have difficulty tolerating distress in their children and in doing so can inadvertently invalidate their child's emotional pain, saying something like 'That is rubbish! Look at how clever and pretty you are – you can't mean that you are worthless!' The irony of such a statement is that it emphasises how the person themself and their thoughts and feelings are discounted and rejected.

It is important for you to try to validate Edi's feelings, experience and perceptions by thinking of the eating disorder as an illness of the emotions. Rather than trying to argue logically with the eating disorder thinking, try to coach in more emotional intelligence, i.e. for

Edi to have that experience and to feel the pain of it but to have the courage to work through it. Help Edi to keep trying to connect, perhaps with a changed goal, rather than withdraw and avoid that experience and the associated pain.

S – Sharing and Support	A warm, loving, supportive atmosphere is the key to overcoming an eating disorder – often difficult to achieve, given the hostility and rejection frequently displayed by the sufferer towards anyone close who spends time in his or her company. (Carers may find it helpful to remind themselves that Edi is expressing and projecting unhappy feelings about the world in general – and you unfortunately happen to be standing in the firing line!)

Share in non-eating disorder behaviours and activities, perhaps a hobby, such as tapestry or painting, puzzles such as crosswords, cards or board games. Fathers and siblings can have a core role here. |

Directive Elements in Motivational Interviewing

In addition to the principles embodied in LESS, motivational interviewing also has some more directive elements, using strategies that help Edi move towards greater readiness to change by creating questions in his or her mind between the status quo – in which the eating disorder forms the individual's identity – and their own deeper ideals, values and ambitions. Chapter 7, 'Understanding Change' concentrates on this aspect.

Communication Skill 2: Tackling Conversation Traps

It is all too easy to fall into a reciprocal, reassurance-giving, trap. What do we mean by reassurance traps? Answering questions about shape are common ones: 'I won't get fat will I?' 'I won't be able to stop eating will I?' 'You haven't put oil in that casserole have you?'

People with an eating disorder have high levels of anxiety and they can look to carers to provide reassurance. The problem with giving Edi constant reassurance is that: (1) the relief in anxiety is only temporary – self-doubt and anxiety soon rage again; (2) Edi does not learn that she or he, the individual, can master fear and doubt and is locked into a dependent relationship – Edi comes to rely on others to reduce anxiety and to check out thoughts. Carers can become locked into providing the pouch (Kangaroo) so that the eating disorder symptoms flourish.

It is harmful rather than helpful to have prolonged discussion about the details of food or weight or shape or negativity. It merely adds validity to the ideas. Sidestep this. Here are some suggestions to sidestep food and weight talk:

- *'It sounds as if your anorexic anxiety is strong.'*

- *'You seem frightened.'*

- *'That is your eating disorder speaking to you.'*

- *'Be brave; it will pass.'*

- *'I have read that if I reassure you it will keep your fear flourishing.'*

- *'If I join in with food or weight talk I will lock you deeper into your eating disorder.'*

- *'I do not enter into discussions about food or calories. We will change the subject.'*

- 'As we have discussed, speaking to the "Eating Disorder" voice is harmful.'

- 'I will listen to you talk to me for five minutes about food/weight/shape, but that will be it for the day.'

- 'It sounds as if you might be confused about making changes . . .'

Communication Skill 3: 'Mind Physiotherapy'

ACTION POINT ➤

Games and activities that 'tone up' a bigger-picture style of thinking, or physiotherapy for the mind, help focus thinking away from eating disorder concerns, perhaps, for example, 'What the Papers Say' – extracting through discussion the gist of a newspaper or magazine article that appeals – or card or board games. Discussion of diagrams or images can also be used to structure conversations in a positive direction.

Stepping back to see the bigger picture is helped by practising skills such as constructing sound bites, headlines, text messages. Think up some metaphors. Try to make these into a light-hearted game.

The ability to be adaptable is another aspect of brain function. Introducing 'planned flexibility' through non-ED activities in family and Edi's life can be a means of bolstering an identity which can embrace change. In your individual family situation, how can a home environment be set up so that there is an opportunity to do things differently? In therapy we suggest that people can challenge themselves by coping with chance, e.g. setting up tasks related to the throw of a die or opening sealed envelopes – you might be able to try this as a form of game.

It is better to introduce flexibility into non-food areas of life first, e.g. taking different routes to work at varying times; wearing something different, a hat or scarf; listening to a different TV or radio channel; then try within the food domain. Here are some examples:

> *Rather than continuing to eat only strawberries for breakfast Jane played a form of 'Simon says' and added whatever her mother was eating that morning.*
>
> *Rather than eating the same snack in the same time and place, Susan agreed to find something to eat within an hour of snack time, no matter where the family were.*

Communication Skill 4: Atmosphere

One of the most important elements families can promote is to ensure *a warm atmosphere at home*, with as little criticism and hostility as possible. It is important that any negative comments about eating disorder behaviours and their effect on Edi and other family members be made *calmly and gently*, through *I think* and *I feel that . . .* comments, rather than by direct accusation.

As outlined in Chapter 4, many carers – especially parents – blame themselves, feeling that they have somehow failed to protect their loved one. Unfortunately many older textbooks about eating disorders even encourage this self-recrimination. Guilt and self-blame are unhelpful and inaccurate. Furthermore, they are dangerous concepts as they can lead to anxiety and depression.

The following feelings can often trigger unhelpful emotions:

- *Shame and stigma*: The symptoms of anorexia nervosa eating disorder are highly visible and clear for everyone to see. They strike at the core of the job as a parent, which is to nurture your child. Carers may feel guilty and ashamed as if it is an overt marker of failure in this. **Correct this misconception – there is no one trigger or explanation. A new 'chaos model' of brain function is that of a soup of random events – often a more helpful explanation.**

- *Anger*: Carers may think that this is just a passing phase and easy to treat, getting angry and frustrated that treatment is slow and not rapidly effective. When you feel you have always done your best and want only to see your loved one well, there is a natural counter-reaction in response to the frequent and extreme outbursts of anger, hostility and rejection – all part of the illness. *Do not rise to the bait and join in with this symptom – remain calm; rather than risk an escalating confrontation, take* **time out** *if and when needed.*

- *Fear*: Carers may be terrified at the physical consequences of the eating disorder. Can Edi's body take the strain? Edi may self-harm in other ways, e.g. by cutting, or taking overdoses. You will fear for Edi's safety. **Accurately assess Edi's medical risks (see Chapter 6). Then, calmly and clearly ask for the resources you need to enable you to manage the situation safely.**

- *Loss*: All the expectations about Edi's future will need to be readjusted. Carers feel devastated about the misery, punishment and deprivation in his or her life, and how the illness affects the whole family. **Work to build and strengthen your relationship on a day-by-day basis. Reassess progress and change on a regular basis – look at the positives, however small.**

Communication Skill 5: Emotional Intelligence

As a carer you want to provide care and safety; it is not easy to show your love with so many negative emotions around. However, outbursts of intense emotion – anger, misery, frustration, grief, emotional pain – with automatic, non-thought-through emotional responses and gut feelings on the surface, are detrimental to setting the scene for change. It is not wrong to have these reactions, but rather it may not be helpful for Edi to see you grappling with these intense, raw feelings. ***Raw emotions can be toxic for someone with an eating disorder who is in an emotionally vulnerable state, feeling uncertain and unskilled in this area.***

Ideally carers need to model 'emotional intelligence'. This means being able to reflect on, digest and move on from emotional reactions. In professional situations this is done by having 'supervision' (or support from someone more experienced, a mentor, and achieving detachment from the situation). For carers, this means having *time to step back and discuss with others what might be happening.*

ACTION POINTS ➡

- It is important to try to process and understand all the strong emotional reactions stirred by an eating disorder within the family. Whenever possible try to set up something similar to 'supervision' for yourself with friends, relatives or other carers (if you cannot find a self-help group nearby, perhaps help to start one?). Spend time with trusted, wise, close others exploring your feelings/beliefs/attitudes and needs – by sharing problems as well as joys, friends will feel able to do the same in their own troubled times. An alternative is to write down your thoughts about the issues involved, which will enable you to explore your feelings more fully. Your thoughts and writing may be shared with others, or not, at a later date. Keeping a journal can be a good way of recording events, thoughts, feelings and reactions, and may also be useful later in reminding of progress.

- In our work with carers at the Maudsley we ask people to spend some time writing about what it is like to live with anorexia nervosa, later sharing these essays and reflecting on their meaning. Once these emotions and what they are trying to say are understood, and have been evaluated as to whether they are based on realistic appraisal or not, then decisions can be made about how to act on them. You may find that taking time to write things down will help you understand why, how and in what way you are upset. Once you can reflect on your thoughts as a compassionate observer, who can look from all sides of the argument, you may be able to see your way forward.

- It is helpful to practise – either alone or with a friend – a few phrases which you can have ready for situations which might lead you to behave in an emotionally unintelligent way, e.g. when you feel overwhelmed by a quick and angry response to one of Edi's outbursts. These phrases may be practised with a supportive friend or family member, so that they are there when needed and ready to help you step back and defuse the situation, e.g.

- *'I don't think this is a good time to discuss the matter. Let's talk about it later when we are both calm.'*

- Or *'We've both said what we think, now I'm going to . . .'*

- Or *'My emotions are too intense to think clearly at the moment. Let's come back to it later.'*

Communication Skill 6: Making Rules and Setting Boundaries

Because of the illness, certain existing family rules may have been disrupted and need to be re-established. In order to cope with the demands of the illness, new, different and/or adapted rules may

skills-based learning for caring for a loved one

need to be worked out, agreed and established, e.g. not eating all the food so there is nothing left for other family members for breakfast; not occupying the kitchen and excluding others who want to use it; not dictating exactly what is eaten for dinner and how it is prepared/cooked, etc.

How do you set limits when Edi is so obviously ill? Or, when bingeing and purging are hidden from the outside world, in bulimia nervosa without anorexia, but relationships are equally as affected?

House rules often change when there is illness, any illness, and in particular long-lasting conditions. As an eating disorder is a problem that can last months or years, you need to have rules that you can stick to for a long time. All family members need boundaries — what kind of behaviours are acceptable/unacceptable? Boundaries need to be set out clearly and consistently; a whole-family round-table discussion of what is and is not acceptable can be really powerful. Think of the Cs.

- You need to be firm about your expectations, and be *consistent*.

- When discussing rules and expectations, show respect for each other and remain *calm*.

- Note and praise any progress *(cherish)*.

- When a rule is broken, remind Edi that you know how difficult it is for him or her to overcome eating problems and you are sure she or he will try hard and win next time *(compassion)*.

- Remember — *it is the behaviour of the illness you dislike, not Edi, whom you still love* (charity).

REFLECTION POINTS

1. Think now about appropriate limits and boundaries within your own situation: what appropriate limits and boundaries are needed to safeguard Edi? How will you set about doing it? You and your partner need to agree fully. You need to think about what sort of help you need from each other to stick to these rules over time. Take time to discuss fully your feelings, perceptions and difficulties arising from eating disorder behaviours, and if at all possible agree a joint way forward.

2. Every family has different rules: what are the rules within your household? Think of as many aspects of family life as possible, the day-to-day accepted rules, and how they have been affected by the illness, e.g. who does the cooking? the washing up? and who demands priority over the bathroom? Try to develop rules that are within your power to enforce. Can you explain *why* you think each rule is necessary? It does not have to be a logically argued case but it must have reason behind it.

ACTION POINT

Set aside time for yourself, and other involved close family members, to have a meeting with Edi when you can talk about your feelings and needs as well as giving Edi time to describe what help and support she or he needs and wants from family members. Schedule the meeting so that everyone has time to prepare, to think about what problems they might want to raise.

The following ideas/rules may be useful at just such a meeting:

- Inviting a family friend to act as a 'referee' to prevent emotional storms from derailing the discussion.

- Ensure that everyone has a turn to speak. Maybe this could be a role of the referee or an appointed 'chair'?

- Agreeing on a length of time that any one person may speak for. Perhaps 10 minutes maximum in any one contribution to a discussion?

- When interruptions are made, calmly remind those present that *everyone* will have a turn to speak.

- Encourage those present to adopt a step-by-step approach:

    Step 1 Explain your emotion/belief and attitude

    Step 2 Explain what you need from the other.

    For example, a parent was feeling sick with worry and anxiety about her daughter's health, which had fallen into the amber region on the medical risk form (see Chapter 3). *'I am terrified about your physical health. I need to know that you are getting weighed by the practice nurse on a weekly basis and you are having your medical risk evaluated regularly.'*

Disagreements

Instead of a group 'disagreement' think more of an 'assertive discussion'. All family or group communication will include a certain amount of debate and conflict about all sorts of things. However, in supporting Edi it is even more important to try to avoid conversations becoming derailed by hostility and misunderstandings. Building an atmosphere of warmth and safety, free from destructive or hostile criticism, is essential while at the same time not bending over backwards to keep the peace. Falling into the trap of accepting and being ruled by eating disorder behaviours can impede recovery.

Take note of the following:

- Even a heated exchange is not always a disaster. Try to keep calm, repeat what you feel is important, and then leave the topic.

- If an exchange becomes destructive/hurtful, acknowledge this and try to end it as soon as possible. When calm, return to the issue.

- If after some thought you feel your reaction has been less than helpful, be prepared to accept partial responsibility, for example: *On reflection, I am sorry . . .* By being able to acknowledge and admit our own mistakes, we give others the important message that everyone is wrong at times as well as showing it is OK to be wrong sometimes.

- Time out – if, despite your best efforts, emotions run high, it may be necessary to adjourn the meeting and start again when everyone is calm again. This could be after a 15-minute break, or the next day. Mutually agree on a time.

Medical Rules

'Medical rules' as well as house rules are equally important in the context of eating disorders. At the Maudsley, we have our own set of medical rules. You may like to discuss these rules in addition to house rules with Edi, or together, as a family. The discussion may be a pre-emptive measure or be currently applicable to Edi's health. If the former, then open, honest discussion may serve as a motivational factor for Edi to try to avoid him- or herself deteriorating into a medically at-risk condition.

skills-based learning for caring for a loved one

You can download the medical risk chart from www.iop.kcl.ac.uk/IoP/Departments/PsychMed/EDU/ downloads/pdf/RiskAssessment.pdf

- If the medical risk assessment reveals that there is a danger to health with risk in the 'Alert' column, then inpatient treatment is recommended.

- It is recommended not to leave home and start university if there is either a high current medical risk or the risk of relapse is high.

- Driving is not recommended below a BMI of 15kg/m²*

* It is recommended that you suggest Edi lets the DVLA and their insurance agency know.

Adopting New Rules

Edi may rail against new rules, accusing you of trying to control him or her and using emotional blackmail. In such a situation it is helpful to *sidestep any argument by stating reasons calmly, firmly and clearly* for your thoughts and feelings – you may have to repeat this several times. Remind Edi of what was planned and discussed and *calmly repeat what you want.*

You may need to coach Edi about how to take up the new behaviours, using affirmation and positive framing as much as possible, e.g.

'I know you are a person who does not want to neglect other people's needs. I need you to . . .'

Communication Skill 7: Reframing Unhelpful Thoughts

In order to be an effective carer, having a philosophical and reflective attitude about your own thoughts and assumptions is essential. Particularly as your thoughts, namely anger and frustration towards the eating disorder, can often trigger unhelpful feelings and reactions towards Edi or other family members. These misperceptions may be positively reframed by using optimism and compassion; contributing to an atmosphere of warmth and healing rather than despair and destruction. Not only is feeling angry and frustrated towards the eating disorder damaging to your relationship with Edi, it will also deplete your energy reserves. In turn, Edi will feel guilty – at fault and responsible for all uncomfortable communication between the two of you. The cycle will keep turning *unless you can break it*.

Reframing thoughts is not easy. It is helpful to try to review your own progress in doing this, if possible in discussion with a supportive friend or professional. By thinking about them, discussing them, identifying possible problem areas in your own situation and being alert to these traps, you may be able to avoid them!

Examples are shown in Table 8.1 of how your thoughts, worries and comments may be reframed so that you can be as effective as possible in helping Edi.

Communication Skill 8: Discussing Change and Progress

People with eating disorders are rarely in what may be called 'Action'. This means that large amounts of effort and energy are needed to move an individual on from the 'precontemplation' and 'contemplation' positions, and acknowledge the problem behaviours. It is therefore helpful to accept their mixed feelings – the ambivalence which is part of eating disordered behaviour – rather than trying to argue logically in an effort to persuade, or to have a head-to-head confrontation (remember Rhino!).

Here are some sentence beginnings to help get you started in discussing change and progress. Try to be as positive as possible if you go for the process, focus on the work involved rather than the outcome. You will not sound like Pollyanna:

> 'Sue, you must be pleased that you managed to . . .'
> 'Sue, it can't have been easy to take that step . . .'
> 'Sue, it looks as if we may have been too optimistic with x goal, but if we remember every mistake is a treasure, what can we learn? . . .'

TABLE 8.1 Reframing Unhelpful Thoughts

Unfavourable remarks about Edi's behaviour or personality 'Critical Comments'	More helpful comments
'She hasn't got friends because she has alienated everyone.'	'She has lost all her friends because they could not cope with her illness.'
'She swears – her language is appalling. She even swears at me.'	'Using strong language must help her in some way. Perhaps it's her way of saying "I'm angry with life!" '
'He doesn't tell the truth any more.'	'This illness has made him unable to be honest.'
'He fights me over everything – he is so selfish.'	'The illness dominates all his thinking, and has taken over his life.'
HOSTILITY	
'I think that there is something wrong with her. She used to be pleasant but now she is anxious, nasty and vicious.'	'She is so anxious, fearful and irritable. The eating disorder has meant that the pleasant part of her character is crowded out.'
'She does it to hurt me.'	'This illness is hurting me so much.'
'She enjoys being difficult, she has destroyed the family.'	'This illness has made her more difficult and it has really affected the whole family.'

(continued)

TABLE 8.1   *continued*

Unfavourable remarks about Edi's behaviour or personality 'Critical Comments'	More helpful comments
'He must see how much we are upset. He must hate us.'	'I am upset by the illness. However this illness is about his emotions and not mine and I must be as calm and warm as possible.'

EMOTIONAL OVER-INVOLVEMENT

'I must invest the whole of my life into caring for Edi and making her life better. I must be there for her 24 hours every day.'	'I need to ensure that the atmosphere at home is as warm and calm as possible. I must have some time to nourish myself and the rest of the family otherwise we will get drained and resentful.'
'Food makes her so frightened. I cannot possibly let my husband be firm with her and insist that she eat even a small amount.'	'There are some rules of living that have to be met. We have to eat to live. If she cannot look after her own nutritional needs we have to take over this role.'
	'We have to help her be flexible and adaptable. She needs to master coping with slightly different approaches and rules.'
'He is so uptight about cleanliness – I must let him have sole use of the kitchen so that he can finish his rituals.'	'It is important that I do not collude with Edi in his obsessions as that keeps them going. The kitchen is a common area and must be kept as such.'

DRAMATISATION OF EVENTS

'Seeing her and what she has been through – I have such an ache – I just want to cry all the time.'	'It hurts to see all she has been through. I know I must remain strong for her, and calm to help her heal.'

ACTION POINT ➡️

Think of particular behaviours causing difficulties in your own individual situation, and develop your own Useful Sentences.

Try to stress that the sufferer always has a CHOICE in their own life and that you will respect that choice (although you would not make the same choice in your own life, and may not completely understand someone else's choice).

> 'It's up to you. If you're going to the cinema then you either have to have your snack before you go or after you get back, with dinner. Alternatively, you could not go to the cinema but have your snack at the usual time. You have to decide – it's about making a choice and compromising.'

Small words can often be important. A key word to use often is **AND** rather than **BUT** when validating the mixed feelings Edi has about his or her eating disorder. **BUT** may be seen as rather judgemental. For example:

> 'Part of you says . . . (Edi talk) **and** yet part of you wants . . .' (a bigger non-eating disorder life)
>
> 'On the one hand you think . . . (Edi talk) **and** on the other hand you . . .'
>
> 'When you focus on you and the eating disorder in this moment, you feel . . . **and** when you reflect on the bigger picture . . .'
>
> 'Zooming in on now, you . . . **and** if you take the broad life perspective you . . .'

The use of **now, yet, at this moment** keeps the idea of change as a realistic possibility. These small words can help bring people back from extremes:

'You do not think you are ready to . . . **yet**'

'At the moment you feel it's too difficult . . .'

Try to be respectful and to offer help in an open way, i.e. do not step in to give advice or generate all the solutions:

'I'd like to spend some time discussing/reflecting with you about . . . When would be a good time for you? Is just now a good time?'

'I'd like to help. Tell me what I can do to help.'

Try to maintain an optimistic tone:

'Tomorrow is a new day – didn't beat it this time, try again tomorrow!'

'I have every confidence in you that tomorrow, you can make things happen differently.'

'I was pleased that you tried. That means that we have gained knowledge.'

Try to find and practise your own Useful Sentences to help you grab any and every opportunity to support, encourage and motivate.

We hope that you will be able to avoid the following traps:

1. Dismissing or criticising other family members' experiences and actions
2. Failing to take the feelings and concerns of other family members seriously
3. Insisting on the correctness of your view of the problem which another family member does not accept (better to agree to differ)
4. Not listening and attending
5. Not providing support to other family members because your energy is so taken up with trying to help and support the person with an eating disorder
6. Falling into reassurance traps with eating disorder behaviours
7. Not recognising areas of competence, forgetting to give praise where due
8. Giving advice without first getting permission to do so
9. Not accepting that it will be in Edi's hands whether she or he works to get better or not.

ACTION POINTS

Things to practise:

- Maximising emotional intelligence
- Remaining calm, consistent and compassionate
- Listening well
- Being clear, kind and persistent about what you want.

Reference List

1. Miller, W., Rollnick, S. *Motivational interviewing: Preparing people to change addictive behaviour.* New York: Guilford, 1991.
2. Miller, W., Rollnick, S. *Motivational interviewing.* New York: The Guilford Press, 2002.
3. Rollnick, S., Mason, P., Butler, C. *Health behaviour change.* Edinburgh: Churchill Livingstone, 1999.

9

Interpersonal relationships

This chapter focuses on the effects an eating disorder has in terms of life situations and relationships and how some of these patterns can keep the illness going.

Eating Disorder as a Form of Non-verbal Communication

Eating disorders are often perceived as discrete, subtle and silent conditions. Not so. The message a sufferer sends out is loud, crystal clear and speaks volumes. **Individuals** may suffer in silence – hidden feelings, dismissed emotions and neglected thoughts – but their message is one of the most powerful examples of non-verbal communication known. Close others instinctively respond, maybe not initially, or even after some time, but, eventually, a response will be triggered . . .

In the initial stage of the illness some of the symptoms of the eating disorder may be seen by family, friends and society as positive – a slim figure, for example, which will be complimented, and focused on striving for achievements in sport, dance or exams, for which they will be praised. This is shown in Figure 9.1 where high expectations imposed by themselves and perhaps added to by others on top of a personality where there is a fear of failure or making a mistake leads to stress. This anxiety narrows the focus and a rigid, detailed approach on perfectionist goals, including those related to food or shape, can win social approval. This type of pattern can occur in all forms of eating disorder.

Striving to do Personal Best is a common trait in people with an eating disorder. When the illness develops, these traits become exaggerated and the 'personal best' becomes unrealistic – trying always to achieve 100 per cent, first place, gold medal, size 0, with everything else seen as failure. Anorexia nervosa's (AN's) ability, in the sufferer's eyes, of helping him or her to achieve these successes, whether academic, sporting or musical, explains the strongly held pro-illness belief: *my eating disorder makes me special*. The individual may additionally consider themselves as special – they are able to do what most of the population strives to do but fails at abysmally – diet. And, moreover, they are good at it. Again, fitting with the pro-eating disorder belief '*my eating disorder makes me special*'. However, in some cases, Edi's self-esteem drops to low levels – she or he may feel that it is impossible to achieve in any way and therefore there is no point in even trying. As they give up and retreat further into themselves, despair and depression set in.

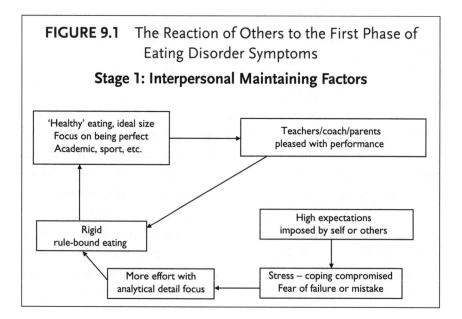

FIGURE 9.1 The Reaction of Others to the First Phase of Eating Disorder Symptoms

Stage 1: Interpersonal Maintaining Factors

skills-based learning for caring for a loved one

The overt physical signs of starvation or of changes in eating patterns and other associated behaviours can lead to a concerned attitude from others. In AN, emaciation and physical frailty send a clear signal to outside observers that something is seriously wrong. It is a powerful sign. People become drawn in to try to help the vulnerable invalid. Here, the pro-eating disorder belief '*Anorexia nervosa communicates distress*' comes to the fore.

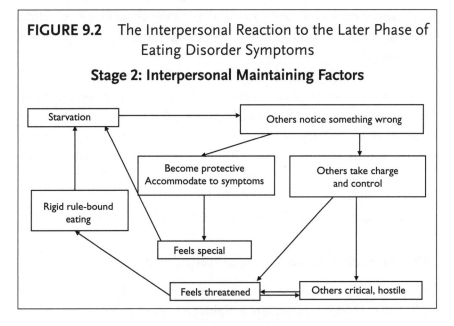

FIGURE 9.2 The Interpersonal Reaction to the Later Phase of Eating Disorder Symptoms

Stage 2: Interpersonal Maintaining Factors

Here other people's concern leads to a change in their behaviour. They may either become protective like the Kangaroo and accommodate to the symptoms, which can reward Edi who likes the special attention and continues with the behaviour or alternatively people may step in to interrupt the behaviour and take control. Edi then feels threatened and resists change. This in turn is frustrated by others who may become critical and hostile, adding to the sense of threat which can escalate into a vicious circle. Stress and any threat increases the rigid rule-bound eating – another trap.

Where bulimia nervosa develops alone, perhaps as a compulsive part of a diet after hearing or reading comments about 'the ideal figure', and without the drive for extreme thinness associated with anorexia, similar negative emotions are part of the picture. Although some of the behaviours are done in secret it is unusual for close others not to realise that something strange is going on even if what is seen is only preoccupation with food, shape or weight. When the compulsion increases to several times a day, Edi feels great disgust at his or her lack of self-control. They are a failure. Feelings of shame and guilt for taking the family's food, and possibly money to fund binges, shoplifting, creating mess around the house and distressing other family members soon develop.

Whatever the eating disorder, or individual mix of eating disorders, carer responses are similar – a mix of helpful and unhelpful reactions. As described in Chapter 4, 'Which Kind of Carer Are You?', Ostrich will try hard to keep the peace by avoiding acknowledgement of the problems, Rhino will try logical arguments, Kangaroo will try to protect. You may have already identified some of these behaviours in yourself. This chapter builds on these metaphors, offering skills to overcome these instinctive reactions.

Interpersonal Factors Can Maintain the Illness

Trying to help someone with a severe eating disorder can feel rather like trying to walk on a tightrope. It is easy to fall into a reaction in which you display either too much or too little of an emotional response, or be overly directive, or underplay the effects on carers and family and try to 'do it all' for Edi. If you are not successful in getting the right balance, it is easy to fall into the snake pit of keeping the eating disorder going.

Getting the Emotional Balance Right

Too Much Emotion – the Jellyfish

High levels of stress in carers are common (Chapter 5, 'Stress, Strain and Developing Resilience'), and coping with that stress for long periods often leads to carers developing their own emotional problems. Every family member is drawn into the situation. This in turn can adversely affect being able to support the sufferer effectively.

The Jellyfish metaphor is useful to describe being in a raw emotional state with all feelings close to the surface (see Figure 9.3 below), for example, dissolving into tears and misery, or becoming frozen with fear, agitated with doubt, uncertain and constantly checking up on Edi. Alternatively, you may erupt into rage. (Edi also may be beset with intense emotional responses.) These intense, visible reactions have an impact on everyone in your environment. Also, Jellyfish may get swept away by currents.

FIGURE 9.3   Emotional Response Too Transparent

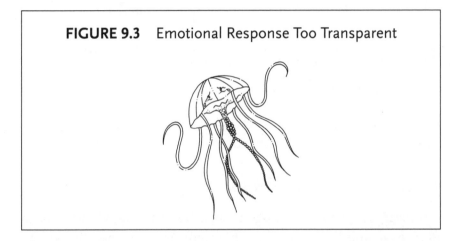

Heightened family reactions to behaviour caused by the illness add to the sufferer's difficulties. She or he may experience them as being rejected by the family, feeling shameful and to blame. Despite knowing that the behaviour is causing distress, she or he seems unable to change it. Sufferers may withdraw completely from family life. Rather than helping a sufferer, a high emotional response may lead to an *increase* in eating disorder behaviours.

As discussed in Chapter 8, 'Communication', it is very important to process and try hard to rise above your own emotional reactions. The skills in Chapter 10 will help you to make a start but you may need additional, sometimes professional, input in order to help your loved one effectively.

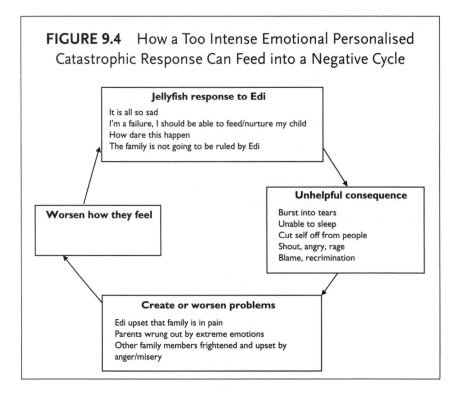

FIGURE 9.4 How a Too Intense Emotional Personalised Catastrophic Response Can Feed into a Negative Cycle

Jellyfish response to Edi

It is all so sad
I'm a failure, I should be able to feed/nurture my child
How dare this happen
The family is not going to be ruled by Edi

Unhelpful consequence

Burst into tears
Unable to sleep
Cut self off from people
Shout, angry, rage
Blame, recrimination

Worsen how they feel

Create or worsen problems

Edi upset that family is in pain
Parents wrung out by extreme emotions
Other family members frightened and upset by anger/misery

Too Little Emotion – the Ostrich

However, some carers swing to the other extreme, attempting to disengage and cut off from the problem. They feel heartbroken to see Edi so ill, in great distress and possibly in poor physical health. They know that talking about food and other pertinent issues will cause further upset. By trying to ignore the problems, like Ostrich, with its head in the sand, carers run the risk of their own behaviour colluding with the eating disorder. (Edi her- or himself uses lots of avoidance ostrich behaviours.)

Some family members may find it difficult to cope with all the problems and emotions at home, and try to avoid them by staying away as much as possible, for example at work, in hobbies or activities outside the home, socialising with friends, perhaps at a pub or club. This means leaving others struggling to shoulder even more of the care burden. The 'Ostriches' find they have to

skills-based learning for caring for a loved one

live with high levels of guilt. As with the too-intense Jellyfish emotional response, the Ostrich also allows the eating disorder symptoms to worsen and the family becomes even more lonely and isolated.

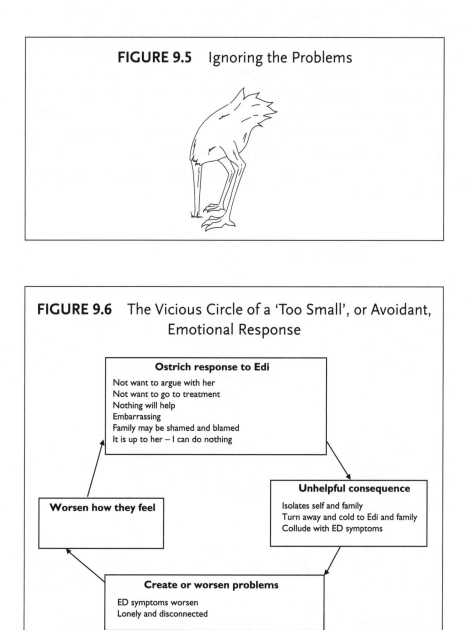

FIGURE 9.5   Ignoring the Problems

FIGURE 9.6   The Vicious Circle of a 'Too Small', or Avoidant, Emotional Response

Ostrich response to Edi

Not want to argue with her
Not want to go to treatment
Nothing will help
Embarrassing
Family may be shamed and blamed
It is up to her – I can do nothing

Unhelpful consequence

Isolates self and family
Turn away and cold to Edi and family
Collude with ED symptoms

Create or worsen problems

ED symptoms worsen
Lonely and disconnected

Worsen how they feel

Too Little Direction – the 'Kangaroo Care' Response . . . Trying to Do It All for Edi

When someone is obviously so ill, unhappy and distressed, it is very easy to be drawn into trying to protect completely in an effort to help, to create a 'pouch' of care to keep ordinary problems and experiences at bay for the sufferer. (Edi may also be highly sensitive to threat – as Kangaroos often are.) Also, Kangaroos often share high standards with Edi – in this case they have high standards and expectations about the parenting role. Rather than *guiding* Edi about choices and possible courses of action, this overprotective response takes away the opportunities to develop and explore the world. It has a reciprocal effect on the person with the eating disorder, who becomes an ostrich, avoiding his or her responsibilities.

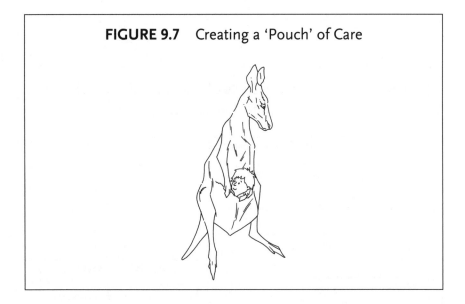

FIGURE 9.7 Creating a 'Pouch' of Care

This type of reaction is common for people who have prolonged periods of face-to-face contact, including nurses on inpatient units. At home, some carers may try to become 'super-carers' and sacrifice themselves to help the sufferer – willing to drive for miles to find the 'right' brand of cereal, available to talk for hours at any time regardless of other matters needing attention, organising work for Edi, paying off bills, spending hours looking for the perfect flat and possibly flatmates for the sufferer . . . and so on. But rather than helping, these well-intentioned, and exhausting, efforts often have the opposite effect. Edi may come to the conclusion that it is their illness that 'rewards' them with this attention and special treatment. They believe that without the illness they would not be protected, doted on, given time, etc. and are reluctant to give up the illness in view of these positive benefits. By adhering to Edi's needs, a carer further reinforces the dependency and lack of responsibility created. This is followed by even greater demands for care . . . leading again to even greater efforts by the carers . . .

Accommodating Edi's behaviour may leave him or her in total control. They may begin to dictate and influence any number of the following:

- The type of crockery used at meals
- How crockery is cleaned
- What time food is eaten
- What place food is eaten
- Exactly what is eaten
- What foods are kept in the house
- How the kitchen is cleaned
- How food is stored
- How food is prepared – cooking and ingredients
- How much and what exercise they take
- How their body shape or weight is monitored
- How the house is cleaned and tidied
- What other family members do and for how long in the kitchen

- What other family members do in other rooms in the house, and at what times

- What other family members can talk about in front of her or him.

In an effort to be a peacemaker, carers may choose to ignore the aspects of Edi's behaviour that impinge on family life. For example, if Edi suffers with bulimia, nothing may be said in spite of food disappearing, money being taken and kitchen and bathroom areas being left in a mess.

Or, carers may get caught up in prolonged ruminations and endless discussions centred around 'eating disorder talk'. They give reassurance in an attempt to relieve Edi's panic-stricken state about whether:

- She or he will get fat

- It is safe or acceptable to eat a certain food

- She or he looks fat in certain clothes

- She or he is ugly/unloveable/selfish/boring/useless/unintelligent, etc.

These super-efforts, added to exhaustion, may lead eventually to burnout for the carer, or understandable breakthroughs of human frustration and anger, especially when other members of the family may be protesting about neglect of their needs (**consistency and calmness** exits). This then leads to the sufferer feeling unsure of reactions which seem to swing between super-care and protection, and inexplicable (to the sufferer) sudden withdrawal of the same. The sufferer then retreats further into his or her eating disorder, rigidly sticking to eating disorder 'rules' in an attempt to avoid their own negative feelings.

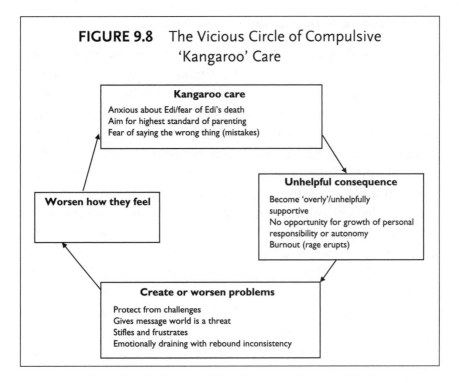

FIGURE 9.8 The Vicious Circle of Compulsive 'Kangaroo' Care

Kangaroo care
Anxious about Edi/fear of Edi's death
Aim for highest standard of parenting
Fear of saying the wrong thing (mistakes)

Unhelpful consequence
Become 'overly'/unhelpfully supportive
No opportunity for growth of personal responsibility or autonomy
Burnout (rage erupts)

Worsen how they feel

Create or worsen problems
Protect from challenges
Gives message world is a threat
Stifles and frustrates
Emotionally draining with rebound inconsistency

Breaking out of a Kangaroo Care Role

It is not easy to break out of this vicious cycle. You may need to reduce your own expectations of what you offer – in other words, step back and close the pouch a bit! This is not only necessary to avoid burnout, but also to help the sufferer work towards regaining some independence and responsibility in life. If someone remains enclosed, with everything done for them on demand, they will *never find out what they can do*. Loss of self-esteem is an important trigger for the illness, but remaining enclosed in that pouch means never having the opportunity to regain lost confidence and rebuild self-esteem. Overcoming obstacles and problems for oneself, no matter how small, is the most successful booster for confidence.

Too Directive a Response: Rhinoceros Response

'Rhinoceros Response' involves trying to present logical arguments to Edi as to why she or he should change, either through coercion, in a determined effort to make the sufferer see the error of their ways, or by presenting ways in which Edi should change. This may arise if you have a rather detailed analytical approach to problem solving (these traits can be genetic and may match those of Edi). All the time, the carer tries to direct these changes. Rather than helping, the response can drive Edi further into eating disorder behaviour by giving opportunities to rehearse and articulate arguments for NOT changing. The eating disorder, *which does not respond to logic*, persists. While the carer will be left feeling defeated, frustrated, drained and angry, Edi will leave these battles victorious with renewed power and energy. At the same time, Edi may be left feeling rejected, unloved, not understood or contemptuous; someone close to them, whom they trust, has dictated forcefully how exactly and why they should change.

FIGURE 9.9   Using Threats, Aggression and Bullying to Pursue their Cause

Often a Rhino's response to failure is to renew efforts and persist. With eating disorders, this soon leads to a spiral of coercion, with the carer increasingly frustrated and angry. With this spiralling coercion is a perception of the carer using threats, aggression and bullying to pursue their cause – all completely ineffective. Other family members may react to the frustration by becoming sarcastic or teasing and mocking the rituals.

Generally it is *not* helpful to argue or coerce people with eating disorders into changing their minds. Their beliefs are rigidly held with strong and abnormal emotional meaning (this is visibly illustrated by brain scan results[1,2,3]). Rather, it is important to calmly agree to disagree, and assertively implement clear limits and boundaries.

The psychological rule of resistance is: *If you order and direct people to change when they are not ready to do so, it can have the opposite effect, i.e. they dig their heels in – a counter-motivational effect.*

This is especially true in eating disorders where beliefs, no matter how distorted they seem to anyone else, are rigidly held. Surprisingly, extreme examples of coercive behaviour amongst professionals have been seen on ED inpatient wards. Where isolation, deprivation, lack of privileges and nasogastric feeding have all failed to entice the sufferer to give up their illness, the staff have resorted to encasing arms in plaster. Innocently, all these measures are done in an effort to save life, to care and in the sufferer's 'best interest'. Unfortunately, such measures also serve to create extreme resentment in the sufferer, who still will not change her or his behaviour on release.

There is a natural human reaction to rebel if you think that your freedom is being curtailed. Thus a common response if someone tries to force you to change your mind is to become more firmly determined not to. The person with eating disorder feels that she or he is not being listened to and becomes more aroused and irritable.

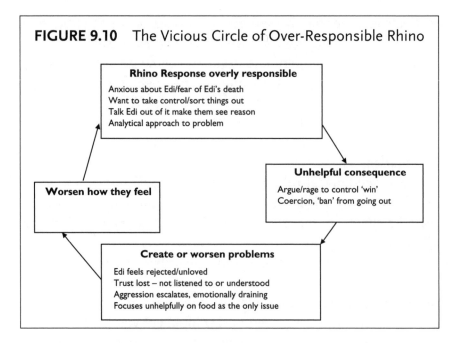

FIGURE 9.10 The Vicious Circle of Over-Responsible Rhino

Rhino Response overly responsible
Anxious about Edi/fear of Edi's death
Want to take control/sort things out
Talk Edi out of it make them see reason
Analytical approach to problem

Unhelpful consequence
Argue/rage to control 'win'
Coercion, 'ban' from going out

Worsen how they feel

Create or worsen problems
Edi feels rejected/unloved
Trust lost – not listened to or understood
Aggression escalates, emotionally draining
Focuses unhelpfully on food as the only issue

Escaping 'Rhino Responsibility'

Try to step back and agree to differ.

> *'I don't see things the way you do, I can't agree with you. But I accept that's how you feel.'*

Walk away from arguments calmly.

> *'I can see you are upset/angry just now – let's discuss this later when we are both calm.'*

Let be, do not join in . . . Not easy – this applies to all coping styles!

Relationship with Siblings and Friends

With eating disorders commonly appearing in teens and early twenties, there may be other siblings in the family. Parents, focused on doing everything they can to support the ill young person, may struggle to help other children in the family who also need time or attention. Siblings may be uncertain how to respond to someone who has lost the ability to join in, whose thinking is distorted and often illogical, has lost his or her sense of humour and fun and doesn't want to join in activities shared in the past. This is also true of friends.

When friends and siblings are unsure how to respond and may be afraid of saying the wrong thing, they may stay away. The sufferer becomes isolated, losing support structures and a sounding board to check out ideas. The distorted eating disorder thinking thus dominates more and more.

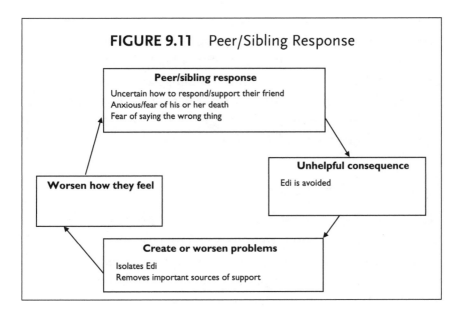

FIGURE 9.11   Peer/Sibling Response

Peer/sibling response
Uncertain how to respond/support their friend
Anxious/fear of his or her death
Fear of saying the wrong thing

Unhelpful consequence
Edi is avoided

Worsen how they feel

Create or worsen problems
Isolates Edi
Removes important sources of support

These patterns are often difficult to break. Depending on the age of siblings and friends, sometimes parents can offer appropriate information, skills and support. In some cases it may be helpful for siblings – perhaps along with the sufferer – to discuss with professionals their worries and concerns about how to offer support. Again dependent on age, siblings may be part of round-the-table family conferences when the problems caused for the family by the eating disorder (for instance, the problems of access to the only bathroom in the house, especially at 'peak times') are discussed openly. Young people, when given the opportunity, can often come up with very practical suggestions.

Sometimes the personality makeup and the associated values of siblings can diverge so much that being bosom friends is impossible. Having too high an expectation about what to expect from siblings may cause problems. Family members may need to step back and see the bigger picture – there will be a lifetime for a relationship but it may be necessary to have your needs for intimacy and warmth met by others.

Siblings and friends can be an invaluable resource in helping Edi gradually regain an understanding of non-eating disorder life and activities, starting with short periods of shared activity, e.g. perhaps watching a short TV programme together, doing a jigsaw, playing cards/a board game, then gradually building up time together. It has been found helpful if siblings and peers are taught reflective listening skills along with other family members – the 'LESS is more approach' (see Chapter 8 about processing emotion and problem-solving skills).

Finding the Right Balance

The most effective treatments for eating disorders have been found to involve all family members working together to help their loved one. Getting alongside to encourage and support the sufferer's efforts and offering praise wherever possible for all efforts and achievements do wonders in recovery.

The 'Just So' Balance of Emotional Reaction – the 'St Bernard' Approach

When your emotions are welling out or fizzing, try to step back, put the emotion somewhere else (in your toe and watch it, or take yourself somewhere else on the ceiling or in a safe calm place so you can watch yourself from above or on a screen). Switch into emotional intelligence mode. Listen and tune into the pain and cry for help of Edi. Summon up the image of a St Bernard dog. Do not join in and shout and rage – you may cause an avalanche. Do not get paralysed by loss and despair and turn away, avoiding tackling the problem. Set out to reach Edi before she or he gets lost further in the frozen wastes of the eating disorder. You can provide warmth, and nurture and can stay with them until change occurs.

FIGURE 9.12   Providing Warmth and Nurture until Change Occurs

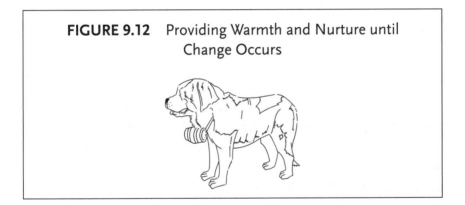

The St Bernard is reliable, steady and dependable by nature, even when a situation is treacherous. The St Bernard's loyalty and compassion are infinite – even after battling in gale-force conditions he can offer love, and protection. He is warm, soft and comforting. He remains calm, collected and follows the job he has been trained to do. Similar to caring for Edi, extra input is often needed.

The 'Just So' Balance of Mentoring – the 'Determined Dolphin' Approach

Dolphins have been recorded swimming alongside boats to guide them through difficult straits, and helping swimmers in the water get to safety. Following on from the descriptions of Kangaroo Care, Rhino Response and Ostrich Approach (possibly carers may think of other recognisable patterns of behaviour), perhaps families could think of a Determined Dolphin helping their loved one towards the safety of recovery . . .

FIGURE 9.13   Gentle Nudging and Guidance from Behind

This means having a good balance of warmth and guidance, sometimes getting ahead of Edi to lead through a safe passage, at other times it may require gentle nudging and guidance from behind. Dolphin as a guide is there alongside the struggling person, trusting their ability to swim out of the situation, sometimes, for example, while listening, remaining behind to allow Edi to take the lead, or moving ahead, being a little more directive when outlining good life choices. Mostly, however, Dolphin will be gently nudging, staying close, watching closely, remaining alongside until the person reaches safety. Then, Dolphin will leave the person to continue on their way, the main aim being that person's well-being.

As in life, setbacks will, of course, be inevitable in the struggle against the illness, and carers can play an essential part in encouragement to keep on trying, with recognition and praise for all efforts:

'Well done! I can see you tried really hard, you'll do even better next time.'

1. *Beware* of falling into an extreme emotional reaction – the Jellyfish or Ostrich. Carers need to remain **calm, warm, nurturing** and **consistent, like a St Bernard**.

2. *Beware* of getting too frightened and drawn into accommodating eating disorder behaviour, being controlled and bullied by it – Kangaroo. It is impossible to hold this position **consistently** – at times Kangaroo will rebound with an emotional backlash (lose your **calm**).

3. *Using logical, analytical, detailed argument* is also unhelpful, or irony, sarcasm or mockery – Rhinoceros. No matter how good the intentions and motivation, trying to force someone into doing something will lead to strong resistance. If you argue over the details you will lose sight of the big picture.

4. *Aim to* keep the pattern of interactions as **consistent** as possible over time and between all family members, while guiding like a Dolphin.

5. *Beware* of times when you and/or Edi are tired, hungry or emotionally depleted as you will not have the energy to take a mature perspective. Step back and withdraw if you can.

6. *Mistakes can be treasures.* Learn from mistakes or setbacks. If you have an unfortunate interaction, apologise, move on and get back on track *'I am sorry, I . . . I was tired . . . I should have said/done . . .'*

Reference List

1. Uher, R., Brammer, M.J., Murphy, T., Campbell, I.C., Ng, V.W., Williams, S.C. *et al*. Recovery and chronicity in anorexia nervosa: brain activity associated with differential outcomes. *Biological Psychiatry* (2003), **54**:934–42.
2. Uher, R., Murphy, T., Brammer, M.J., Dalgleish, T., Phillips, M.L., Ng, V.W. *et al*. Medial prefrontal cortex activity associated with symptom provocation in eating disorders. *American Journal of Psychiatry* (2004), **161**:1238–46.
3. Uher, R., Murphy, T., Friederich, H.C., Dalgleish, T., Brammer, M.J., Giampietro, V. *et al*. Functional neuroanatomy of body shape perception in healthy and eating-disordered women. *Biological Psychiatry* (2005), **58**: 990–7.

10

Modelling emotional intelligence and problem-solving skills

Extreme Emotions

People with an eating disorder often find it difficult to manage and regulate emotions. They may try to avoid feeling, thinking about and acknowledging emotions, and sometimes act as if showing or talking about difficult emotions – such as hurt, anger and sorrow – is unacceptable. They may be unable to react verbally and actively at the appropriate time, to the appropriate person, and at the appropriate level. In other words, they may have perfected the *art of avoidance*. At other times their emotional output may be intense and extreme.

Emotions are what make us human and guide our progress through life. The maturation of emotional intelligence is a key part of development. We discussed earlier how this developmental process can get derailed by an eating disorder (Chapter 3).

Therefore a key aspect of treatment is to learn how to manage emotions. Chapter 8, 'Communication', includes discussion as to how carers – who may recognise elements of, for instance Kangaroo, Ostrich or Rhino, in their own behaviour – can model adaptive emotional processing for Edi. Carers may recognise that they too need to modify and change a particular response or behaviour. Through modification and effective demonstration, Edi picks up these new skills.

Edi will need help in being able to master the difficulties and risks entailed in communicating negative emotions. Frequently Edi's standard way of being is as a 'people pleaser', leading to feelings that they are unable to control their own lives. Failure to be emotionally honest in a respectful way may lead to a build-up of hurt and anger, feeling useless because their unexpressed inner feelings are so intense and huge. To express such negative feelings may seem disgusting and out of control.

Often the only outlet for these extreme feelings may seem to be in forms of self-punishment, self-abuse, self-starvation, vomiting, laxatives, over-exercise, etc. Physical pain may be more acceptable than emotional pain. Sometimes self-control breaks and the result is bulimia, leading to further feelings of intense disgust, which again they may have difficulty in expressing directly.

An eating disorder can take hold because it comes to serve a function for an individual, who finds that it helps control or dull strong emotions. Starvation may take the edge off the intensity of emotions, making the sufferer 'feel numb', allowing the individual to isolate and suppress the continuous bombardment of negative feelings. By restricting food intake and dulling emotions, sufferers remove themselves from the hurt, pain and injustice in their lives. Other eating behaviours such as bingeing, over-exercising and vomiting may also be a way of trying to soothe or distract from intense feelings. Sometimes patients describe themselves as being 'full'. This fullness is felt as a physical sensation but, in reality, they are actually 'full' of feelings and emotions. Some sufferers deal with the 'fullness' by purging or vomiting, others are unable to eat – they feel enormous, like a balloon, taut and stretched, and cannot fill themselves up any more.

The tendency to avoid emotions happens automatically so that Edi may not even recognise that she or he feels an emotion, and may also be unaware that others might pick up on their non-verbal emotional reaction (a slight blush of the cheeks, a tear in the eye, hesitation in speech, turning away the head or casting down the eyes).

ACTION POINT ➤

Noticing emotions – an emotional 'Geiger counter'

It can be helpful if carers are able to act as an emotional 'Geiger counter' by paying particular attention to and picking up the non-verbal signs of an emotional reaction. Be sensitive to emotional reactions by using skills of empathy and compassion; put yourself in their shoes. Think of what words you might use to describe how they might feel. On registering an emotional reaction, stop, think and try to understand what is happening.

> *'It looks/sounds as if you are upset.'*

Take the time to listen and try to understand the context. Guide Edi through the process of analysing what it going on.

> *'I notice that when I said . . . your eyes became downcast/ you turned your head away. I can see by this that you are either upset or angry in some way. Can you try to tell me more about what you are feeling and thinking?'*

This can then open up a conversation in which Edi may be able to acknowledge what they might need, how they may feel thwarted or rejected by others and how they experience conflict. A conversation avoids both Edi suppressing and internalising his or her emotions, further feeding their eating disorder, and/or an explosion of negative emotion expressed through aggression and rejection avoidance. Talking increases Edi's ability to master emotions and to understand the bigger picture about whether the emotion is signalling something important or whether it is oversensitive mislabelling.

Sometimes talking about specific feelings and emotions is so alien to sufferers that, although they know they are feeling something, usually too much, they cannot describe exactly what. If Edi finds it too hard to express their thoughts, they can identify their feelings through writing. Again, as with the 'Readiness Ruler' used in Chapter 7, having a written piece to start and/or focus a discussion on can sometimes be a useful adjunct.

White Lies

Although Edi has difficulty naming and defining her or his own emotions they may be highly attuned to the non-verbal emotions of others. Thus beware of telling 'white lies', 'no, I am not upset', etc., when you are. If you deny your own emotional response then you are modelling stifling and non-attending emotions. The aim for Edi is to be more intelligent about her or his emotions and not to suppress and deny them. It is a better teaching experience if you own your emotional response and move on to what you aim to do about it:

> 'Yes, I am slightly upset that you lost weight last week after what you told me you would do.'

- **Reset goals.** *I realise that change is difficult and breaking from your habits is tough, I should not hold overly high expectations. I too easily jump to a perfectionistic goal. I need to be more realistic.*

- **Notice glass half full.** *I was pleased when I saw you put some change into action though, by adding toast to your breakfast.*

- **Acceptance.** *It is often impossible to instigate change in the home environment. Many people need hospital treatment.*

- **Soothing.** *I am disappointed that it is so hard. However, there is no point in dwelling on that. Shall we look through the newspaper together and plan an outing this weekend?*

Edi may project his or her own emotional response onto others, for example whilst walking out with their mother Edi passed some old school friends. Edi said, 'You must be ashamed of walking out with me when other people see us and stare.'

An **emotionally unintelligent response** would be to say, '*No of course I am not ashamed of you. You look lovely.*'

This response contains a white lie as the mother is desperately worried about the 10kg weight loss.

A more **emotionally intelligent** response would be to say, '*Do you feel ashamed about your illness when you see old friends?*'

BOX 10.1 Hints for Improving Communication and Coaching in Emotional Processing

1. **Look and listen for signs of anger and hurt**, e.g. going quiet, eyes down, flushed, tears in eyes, micro-movements in eye, nose or mouth that register the flash of an emotion, or breaking flow of conversation. Validate the emotion, e.g. '*It looks to me as if . . .*', '*I may be wrong but you seem . . .*', '*Often when people have an expression like that they feel . . .*'

2. **Encourage Edi to voice the difficulty**. Is it hurt, disgust or anger? Ask Edi to talk about what they feel at the moment. '*What are you thinking?*', '*Would it be helpful to talk about it a bit?*' or '*Might it be a good idea to reflect on it a little?*' If they cannot find words to express and describe their feelings, encourage them to think about which of the core emotional states they are in. Do they feel abandoned and alienated, are they frightened or are they craving for some resource?

3. **Listen carefully to the painful thoughts**; do not prematurely brush them off or reassure – it is shaming and humiliating to have your feelings and fears brushed aside (e.g. *'Don't be silly! Of course you don't need to be scared of that!'* or *'You are being ridiculous! You shouldn't get offended by things like that!'*). **No matter how differently from Edi you may feel, try to put yourself in Edi's shoes.** Try to understand what they are saying and to pick up the underlying message which the sufferer may have difficulty in expressing directly.

4. **Do not over-identify with Edi's feelings**, or get overwhelmed by your own reaction to what he or she might be feeling, i.e. their sadness or victory is not your sadness or victory. ***Take a step back and remain the carer.***

5. **Ensure that you don't get into a self-defensive pattern**; be grown up about any negative feedback yourself – take it on the chin and, if necessary, be prepared to say sorry or offer reparation. If you do not understand the particular feelings (because you do not share the sufferer's view of whatever event has caused a problem) perhaps you could say, *'Thank you for explaining how you see things. I'm sorry you feel that way and you feel upset/angry/sad. I see things differently and I'd like to explain how I feel about this . . .'* It is important not to overreact to Edi's emotion, i.e. do not get threatened by their anger, or defensive at their criticisms, hurt by separations, or feeling rejected by their disinterest. Try to react calmly; take a break when needed. *'I'm tired right now, let's talk about this later.'* But, make sure that time is found to do just that – don't say or promise to do anything you can't follow through.

6. **Work to give positive feedback about the ability to express an emotional response.** For example you might say *'I am very impressed that you are able to tell me about your distressing feelings. Well done for having the courage to tell*

me you felt hurt/angry/sad. It's helpful to know how you feel so that we can talk about how we both feel and try to work out how to cope with this situation if it happens in the future.'

7. **Allow Edi to feel emotional pain sometimes** – don't have unrealistic expectations, e.g. want Edi to be happy all the time. (No one can be.) There must be balance between positive and negative emotions – that is the human condition. Positive and negative emotions are the accelerators and brakes guiding us through life and they make us who we are. The challenge is to be able to learn from our emotions and shape our lives accordingly.

8. **Set aside whatever time is necessary to reflect on the emotion calmly and compassionately**. Gently return to the discussion later, if an opportunity presents itself, if further thoughts or observations occur.

Often people with an eating disorder have the tendency to assume that the world and people in it follow logical rules, keep to order, etc. However, with human beings, there are often chaotic and unpredictable feelings which can lead to unexpected and inexplicable events. These make it difficult to mind-read and predict another person's thoughts. That is why it is important to try to use any tools we have to communicate well – both verbal and non-verbal. Exploring emotions and thoughts together helps to develop stronger bonds and closer relationships.

Problem Solving

Once problems and difficult emotions are acknowledged it is possible for you, the carer, to model more appropriate coping skills. This may mean teaching skills such as problem solving or assertiveness. *Always beware of becoming a Kangaroo (over-protective) or a Rhino (overbearing)*. Try to mentor Edi so that she or he learns (or relearns) these effective life skills and gains a sense of mastery. Achieving and the eventual sense of freedom and independence this achievement brings boost Edi's confidence.

You may need some coaching or assistance in order to go through these steps but they are skills that can be applied to many situations.

ACTION POINT →

Coaching Edi how to problem solve

1. *Generate as many ideas/solutions as possible* (even if some are wacky – humour can oil this process). Using a pen and paper can help keep this task open and flexible.

2. *Avoid getting prematurely bogged down in detail*. Keep your eye on the bigger picture, i.e. what are we trying to do here?

3. *Choose between the options* generated in the first stage to find the optimal workable strategy.

4. *Give some guidance or facilitation about how to choose between them*: what resources will we need? Are there any uncontrollable roadblocks?

5. *Encourage breaking the task down* into appropriate-sized steps.

6. *Make a concrete plan* to take one of the options. Practise, role play, script it out in detail to help develop Edi's confidence when approaching actual implementation of the plan.

7. *Plan a review and debriefing session; set a time for it.* Remember – **every mistake is a treasure** and helps us learn. Look at what went well and not so well. Think about and discuss what can be learnt for *next* time.

skills-based learning for caring for a loved one

11

Managing undereating

Introduction

Through this chapter, we hope to be able to guide you, and Edi, through the many challenges eating poses. We work through eating at different stages of the illness in the following time-based format (see Figure 11.1). Of course, not all this chapter may be relevant to you, or Edi, immediately. You may work forwards, and backwards, through the topics as the dynamics of Edi's illness change. If not all pertinent to you at the present, maybe the information contained here will aid your reflection on past progress made or offer hope and promise for future achievements.

The aim of treatment for an eating disorder is to return food and meals to their normal place – as fuel. Furthermore, as eating has a central role within all cultures, providing a backdrop for socialising, celebration and enjoyment, it is an important source of connection. Many of 'life's activities' revolve around food. Reintegrating into life (work, school, relationships, friends, college, etc.) also involves reintegrating into food (birthday dinners, supper invitations, lunch meetings, cooking for friends, picnics, BBQs, etc.). Initially, 'food is fuel' in treatment but, later, and sometimes much later (sometimes years), the aim of treatment is to adapt the sufferer to see food in the context of friends, family, talking and connecting. A tough assignment and frequently imagined as inconceivable.

Thus the goal of helping someone to recover from an eating disorder is to relearn how to:

1. Eat sufficient for the body's needs

2. Eat flexibly and with variety

3. Eat socially – with food set into the context of the bigger picture of life.

A step-by-step approach is used to work towards these goals.

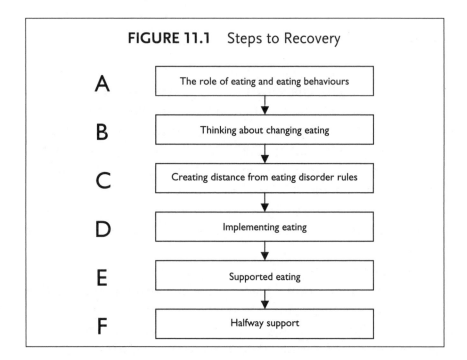

FIGURE 11.1 Steps to Recovery

A — The role of eating and eating behaviours

B — Thinking about changing eating

C — Creating distance from eating disorder rules

D — Implementing eating

E — Supported eating

F — Halfway support

A. The Role of Eating and Eating Behaviours

Eating is Non-negotiable

All living creatures must eat to live – whether to eat or not is a non-negotiable area. The body has a variety of control systems in place to ensure that an individual does not die of starvation – this is one of the basic needs of all living organisms.

skills-based learning for caring for a loved one

Eating disorders, especially anorexia nervosa, where refusal is of every scrap of nourishment and sometimes of liquid, disrupt one of the core aspects of living. However, although eating is a non-negotiable area, the How, Where, When, What and With Whom of food and eating *are* areas that can be negotiated.

As early weight restoration can lead to a shorter illness course, it is important to get on to 'change talk' as soon as possible. When the illness follows a long course, patterns and rituals become deeply ingrained and highly habitual. The longer the illness continues, the harder it is for Edi to contemplate change. 'Change talk' is therefore a priority; the sooner being better.

Carrots and Sticks

We are all designed to be motivated to do things that are rewarded, i.e. that give us pleasure or are 'nice' in some way; and to turn away from things that are not rewarded, i.e. nasty. One of the difficult things to understand is how this principle works in relation to an eating disorder such as anorexia. From the outside it is difficult to imagine how *not* eating could possibly be rewarding in any way. However, it would seem there are some perceived positive benefits for people with anorexia, possibly because there is something unusual in the biological response to starvation. For example, it is as if starvation is somehow uplifting, vitalising and energising to sufferers. A number of secondary effects may also become rewarding or feel somehow pleasurable (for example, attention, care, compliments).

In treatment at the Maudsley, to explore these reasons, we ask people to write a letter to 'anorexia nervosa, the friend'. A questionnaire was developed and over 300 women with AN were surveyed to examine what were the most common negative and positive aspects of their eating disorder. We found that the most common rewards were:

- Anorexia makes me feel safe, secure and in control

- Anorexia is a way of showing my distress

- Anorexia is a way of helping me avoid growing up and what that entails – responsibility.

It is probable that some of these are relevant to your loved one. In order to help Edi change and leave any eating disorder behind, carers will need to help Edi to find other ways to get these rewards, i.e. to:

- Find other ways of helping Edi feel safe, secure and in control. As outlined in previous chapters, one of the best ways of doing this is in an atmosphere in which there is *calmness, consistency, compassion* and love – not easy to create such an atmosphere when everyone is anxious/on edge/walking on egg shells, which is common in families coping with an eating disorder.

- Find other ways of communicating and dealing with distress (coaching in emotional intelligence).

- Find ways of making the experience of taking personal responsibility more positive (coaching to develop skills to face problems and seek solutions; to be more flexible; and to take in the bigger picture).

We have developed a model (shown in Figure 11.2) which attempts to explain how undereating *may* be maintained. In this model, eating and food (or secondary linked features such as weight and shape) become associated with added and unusual meaning and value for Edi. This meaning becomes embedded in the individual's identity, informational processing (rigidity and detailed analytical) and emotional systems (anxiety) which shape the consequent behaviours. This leads to rule-driven eating and avoidance. Eating is decontextualised and is not merely a behaviour used to satisfy hunger, supply essential lubricants or as part of social lubrication and bonding. These rules about eating *may* relate to weight control but frequently they are far more complex. For example, whether an individual feels 'good enough' to

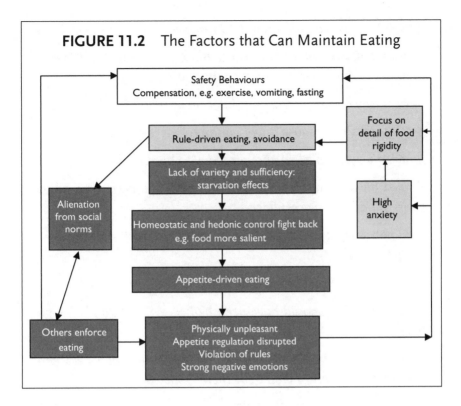

FIGURE 11.2   The Factors that Can Maintain Eating

Safety Behaviours
Compensation, e.g. exercise, vomiting, fasting

Rule-driven eating, avoidance

Lack of variety and sufficiency:
starvation effects

Homeostatic and hedonic control fight back
e.g. food more salient

Appetite-driven eating

Physically unpleasant
Appetite regulation disrupted
Violation of rules
Strong negative emotions

Alienation
from social
norms

Others enforce
eating

Focus on
detail of food
rigidity

High
anxiety

eat or 'merits' the reward of eating food, whether they have worked hard enough or achieved enough to 'earn' a meal, whether they are 'worthy enough' to take up space. The rules may be idiosyncratic, involving some function of food such as colour or aesthetics or the effect on sexuality or performance. Often 'rule-bound eating' rules have complex emotional undertones, which are personal, peculiar, often unfounded and directly related to food and meals.

A few examples of 'food rules':

'I can't eat this, it will make me fat.'

'I can't eat that because it is green.'

'If I eat my food in a clockwise order going round my plate, it makes me less anxious.'

'I have to chew each mouthful 15 times.'

'I must eat the vegetables on my plate first, then the protein, then the carbohydrate. Things cannot be mixed.'

'If I eat any oil my weight will shoot up immediately.'

'I can't eat this because it will poison me, it is red.'

'I haven't accomplished enough today to deserve dinner.'

'I must always leave a tiny bit on my plate – even if it's a single grain of rice, or one cornflake.'

'I do not deserve to eat because I didn't finish task A in the right time.'

'Any food that I do eat must be hot.'

'My exam mark should have been higher. I'm not good enough to eat.'

'Meals have to be on time: breakfast 8.00am, lunch 12.30pm and dinner 6.00pm. I won't eat them if they are late.'

For Edi, following these rules (Edi's own individually developed rules about food and eating) serves the function of reducing anxiety (at least in the short term) especially in individuals with an obsessive compulsive disposition valuing order and control or in those who have high levels of anxiety or who are oversensitive to the reactions of others. Or, Edi may have an analytical eye for detail and reduce food to its elements, e.g. *how many calories, how much fat?* To change from this pattern of eating behaviour, an individual needs to zoom out and be able to see the bigger picture. This involves being able to step back to attain a broader perspective of meaning and value. **Compulsive, anxiety-laden thoughts about food have to be challenged, and it is necessary to work through and tolerate the high anxiety that this will inevitably produce.**

Compensatory or 'Safety Behaviours'

At times Edi takes food only to please and appease others – social cues; or in response to powerful appetite cues – overwhelming hunger; or in an attempt to cover their disordered eating behaviour. This 'non-rule-bound' eating causes high anxiety.

> When my daughter, aged 23, developed anorexia, binge/purge type, she ate a good healthy meal across the table from me each evening. GLS

> I would hate the thought of friends seeing me as weak, pathetic or appearance conscious, the usual eating disorder stereotypes. If ever I had to eat with people I would restrict rigorously beforehand. I would then attempt to eat as normally as possible at dinner and conceal my terror. Panic-stricken after a 'huge' meal, I would walk home (miles) and exercise and restrict the next day to compensate for my indulgence. AC

To cope with this distress, a variety of what are called 'safety' behaviours may develop, e.g. vomiting, misuse of laxatives, over-exercising, or thoughts to try to neutralise the distress which are found soothing, such as: *'Once I am free I will choose how I will eat'*, or perhaps, *'Being made to eat doesn't count'*, etc.

> After she had eaten with me, she went upstairs to her bedroom, saying she wanted to watch TV. On the way to her bedroom she visited the bathroom to get rid of everything she had eaten. GLS

> Later on in my illness, although I still wouldn't feed myself adequately, I started to accept food from my parents. Giving food to myself was too indulgent; I was worthless and undeserving. Accepting food from others was different – the choice was removed and the guilt after eating was alleviated slightly. AC

As they reduce the anxiety caused by eating, these safety behaviours can quickly become reinforced and habitual.

At times, they involve other people to elicit reassurance, e.g.

> Edi: '*If I eat that I will get fat*'.
>
> Response: '*Of course you won't.*'

A repetitive cycle can be set up with the carer providing the safety routine. These exchanges allow Edi to rehearse eating disordered thinking, thereby reinforcing it. Ideally sidestep being invited to join in this dance.

> Response: '*I think you know that we all need food to live. The hospital have told me that I should not provide mindless reassurance so I will not say more.*'

Disentangling the Meanings behind Food and Eating

The aim of treatment is to set the scene so that **the person with an eating disorder develops the skills and motivation to change**; relaxing their rule-bound eating and putting aside their safety behaviours.

Learning and memory is an active process involving brain growth and nerve synapse sprouting; malnutrition produces a reduction in brain growth factors and interferes with learning and active brain function. Thus, a vicious circle develops. When anorexia begins in adolescence, starvation interferes with the development of the 'social brain' and maturation of cognitive functioning. The result is that social, emotional and intellectual development is stunted and remains child-like. The capacity to reflect and the ability to step back and get an overview of emotions, thoughts and behaviours, all of which are essential to recovery, are impaired. Another trap is sprung.

Where anorexia develops at a later stage, Edi seems to regress to a much earlier level of development.

> When she was 23, at very low weight and very ill, my daughter frequently behaved as if she was about 3, with understanding and perceptions of around that age. GLS

> Your decision-making skills disappear. You have to ask for advice, reassurance and permission for everything. You can't interpret other people's reactions or emotions without guidance. You become totally dependent on others to function day-to-day, not just for nourishment, but to live. AC

Although it can be used for short periods to preserve life and improve brain function, forced feeding and attempts to change the eating disordered behaviour by coercion alone will not lead to permanent change. Unless these restricted, rule-bound patterns of eating are modified, they can become habitual and hardwired into the brain.

Therefore, helping someone with an eating disorder involves a balancing act: on the one hand giving the time and help needed to reach a point at which the individual has the motivation to explore and experiment with non-rule-bound eating and reduced safety behaviours; on the other hand, not letting malnutrition and symptoms interfere with brain function by causing brain cell death, disrupting reward pathways, and inhibiting learning and development.

The Body Fights Back – the Bulimic Trap

Extreme tension develops between rule-bound – or instrumental – eating and the physiological cues that control appetite. The body and brain desperately need nourishment to function effectively, and a series of mechanisms to increase appetite fight against malnutrition caused by the starvation. The strength of these innate mechanisms varies between individuals. It is possible that some individuals, genetically predisposed to anorexia nervosa, have a more loosely regulated system. The lifetime memory bank and experience of food, eating and appetite is lost if abnormal eating behaviours persist for any length of time. Thus, the basic concepts of hunger and fullness have to be relearned and gradually trained to take over normal appetite control.

In some individuals the 'reward pathways' become so sensitive that, once eating restarts, it takes a while to shut off. A drive to overeat, with intense urges and cravings, emerges.

A variety of perverse eating behaviours arise when rule-bound eating is at war with the biology of appetite, e.g. picking/stealing foods and binge eating. The response to this drive, and the intense urges and cravings, will vary with the individual. For instance, in the restrictive type of AN, purging behaviours such as vomiting may not be part of the scene; while in AN binge/purge type it may enter the picture at an early or later stage. Chapter 12 focuses on helping to reduce bingeing and overeating behaviours.

B. Thinking about Changing Eating

Insight Using the Nutritional Risk Ruler

In Chapter 7, the use of a 'Readiness Ruler' to aid motivation to change is illustrated. Here, we use the same tool to discuss the balance between motivation to change and objective evidence of nutritional safety. The 'Nutritional Risk Ruler' gauges Edi's insight into the potential impact the illness plays on their medical health as well as their quality of life, both in the short and long terms. **The aim is to initiate a conversation discussing nutritional health.**

Nutritional Risk Ruler:

Unable to ensure nutritional safety   *Maintain full nutritional health*

0-------1--------2-------3------4------5-------6------- 7------8-------9---------10
